eyes

michel serres

Member of the Académie Française

translated by Anne-Marie Feenberg-Dibon

BLOOMSBURY

Iconography: Frédéric Mazuy
Graphic design and layout: Bianca Gumbrecht
Photo-engraving: Les artisans du Regard

First published in French, in 2014 by Le Pommier, with the title : *Yeux*
© Bloomsbury, 2015
ISBN 978-1-4742-6364-1

Michel Serres' book, *Eyes,* is a masterful enactment of ways of seeing, thinking and knowing. Like his previous books, *Music, Living,* and *Statues,* the book itself is the object to guide our vision: through beautifully curated images and text, this book addresses us to a world with a painterly eye, where the painting emits, transmits and emanates its own radiance. It poses the questions, what is it to *see and to be seen*: what if the world sees? How do we imagine eyes other than human eyes: what can insects, animals and seemingly inanimate objects see? How does this reconfiguration of seeing change our perception of the natural world and the human species?

Serres asks us to consider that the "universe is studded with eyes", to revisit caves and caverns, to encourage the wisdom of unknown worlds and images. Philosophers have always been champions of light, but Serres reorients philosophical thinking towards a world of darkness *and* light. And in this fusion of density and light, the world supports a multitude of images that transmit and emit information. This is a world full of networks and connections between animate and inanimate things. Serres observes how a soccer or basketball game is brought together by the marvelous, seemingly-inert object of the ball as it joins or separates its players, this is a network of relationships and these networks exist everywhere and everything "sees"; the power lies in how we envisage these networks and systems.

The world speaks through different eyes. *Eyes,* then, encompasses more than the purely visual. Almost like a philosophy of shadows, this book illuminates from within its pages a way to see, to imagine, to invent, to think. With this comes a dream: to create a museum for the multitude of visions from other species, objects, and things in which the human subject plays only a particular part. This glorious exhibition offers a transformation of perception; it is a radical action and a revolution in thought. It is a challenge to human narcissism just as it is a vision to broaden our respect for the world and all things that inhabit it.

Thinking in the World celebrates a new approach to the study of thinking. More far reaching than the study of "thought" (on the page or in philosophy), the series pursues thinking as it unfolds within the world. Michel Serres' *Eyes* does just that: it pioneers a radical philosophy of thinking and of vision. It is the ultimate "eye-book", an object with which to envisage and navigate the world of networks, relationships and technologies.

Jill Bennett and Mary Zournazi
Series Editors, *Thinking in the World*

For Catherine Boulanger

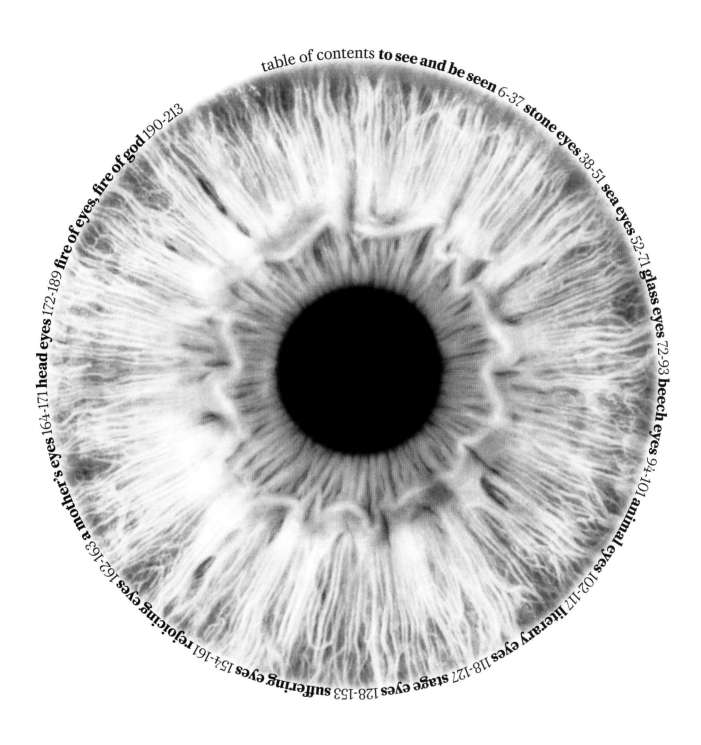

table of contents **to see and be seen** 6-37 **stone eyes** 38-51 **sea eyes** 52-71 **glass eyes** 72-93 **beech eyes** 94-101 **animal eyes** 102-117 **literary eyes** 118-127 **stage eyes** 128-153 **suffering eyes** 154-161 **rejoicing eyes** 162-163 **a mother's eyes** 164-171 **head eyes** 172-189 **fire of eyes, fire of god** 190-213

Esthetics

My ambitious book *Music,* whether a success or failure, tries to answer a naive question: "So what is this paradise whose name is shared by all the muses?" My book does not describe any particular composer or work of a given period, but the art itself, as such. Taking a heroic if mad risk, it speaks the language of wave trains that preceded all language, of sounds that thunder beneath every language and of universal noises that precede meaning. Similarly, my book *Statues* examined the sculptor's majestic gesture in preparation before the fashioning of an object in an art analogous to music. While totally different, *Living* proposed the same risky strategy with respect to architecture.

I have reflected on a few pages written by Balzac, Verne or Hugo without daring to ask the question "What is literature?" Even so, a scattering of my essays describes paintings signed by Carpaccio, Bellini, Poussin and Turner, without ever questioning painting itself.

Will I finally be able to do this here?

For years, I have hesitated between two contradictory theories to interpret Turner's paintings. Either the painter's gaze changes and he no longer sees the same world, and painting itself is changing. Alternatively, the mist and light of the world changed after a gigantic volcanic eruption in the Sunda archipelago and produced a small nuclear winter in Europe. Either the work represents a vision or shows what is seen. The mystery of representation lies between this indetermination and contradiction.

William Turner, *Snowstorm, Avalanche, and Thunderstorm. A scene in the highest part of the Aosta Valley, Piedmont,* 1836-1837, The Art Institute of Chicago.

To see and be seen

Here we go. A work by a great painter lends itself to contemplation
and provokes admiration. More than that, like a face which is seen and sees,
it pierces the wall as a burning gaze would pierce its grey façade.
It glitters with light and meaning, and sees as an eye would see,
even when it is not a portrait. The painting actively floods the room with light
and the viewer with enchanted understanding.
This is perhaps just an image, but it is actually more like a fiery gaze.
Before a painting by Breughel, Rembrandt or Van Gogh...
I am seized by the twofold sensation of discovering and being discovered.
Let me say this: when the painting does not act like an eye,
the image is weak and provides little information.
No, a painter does not reproduce an image on a canvas, but he paints whatever
light the subject matter receives, stores, treats and produces,
in addition to the information it contains.
The work thus becomes not just a receptacle for luminosity
but it also emits, releases and transforms its own luster.
For me, it seems to have the same properties as an active eye.
The master shows me his painting and at the same time the work looks at me.
It is as if the fire of his gaze went through the work, changing it into a vision.

This image is too obvious. Yes, we look at the painting and yes, the face looks at us. We know that the
word *face* means two things; it can see and be seen. This book wants to present a more problematic
intuition, and argues that somehow things themselves have sight. The painter's supreme art would then
consist in representing those views that give the world a strange power to act.

Vincent van Gogh, *Self-portrait with Grey Felt Hat*, 1887-1888, Van Gogh Museum, Amsterdam.

Let me see the world as I believe the artist sees it. Let me imagine that the painter sees things as I see them and as I am seen by them. I would like this book, which will speak of vision, painting and the world, to function like a painting too, that is to say like a gaze. I would like these pages to capture, store, treat and diffuse light like the artist and his painting!

I dream that painting, and even more my book, will imitate the things of the world. I believe that a lake, a sapphire, an ordinary stone, a corner of the sky, a bluish serac, and the sea with its innumerable smiles, the yellow sun or the chromatic face of constellations, the jaguar's streaked coat, the hummingbird's lively flight and Venus's nude body, see me as well or sometimes better than I see them. They receive, store, treat and release light and shine like eyes. Yes, let me dream: since most things return as much light as they receive, trap and treat, I imagine that they see as much as they are seen. I believe I am seen by them and I see myself seen by them.

This image is also too obvious, but both will slowly introduce the subject of this book. Here the face sees; the artist sees the face. Imitative, the work is seen and sees. This game of mirrors is an element in our relationship with the world that continuously multiplies such interaction. What or whom did the imitated painting copy or imitate? And the painted face too, whom did it copy or imitate? Whom or what did it see and whose gaze then changed when seeing it? This labyrinth has no exit.

A copyist at the Louvre.

This image – still too obvious really – throws us into the world's gaze. First, the two frogs with their four eyes seem to hold back as they are almost sliding into a dark eye. They also seem to be freeing themselves. I call *look* the opening allowing us to have access to an oven, an excavation or a sewer for reparations. The ancient Romans had a celebration called *mundus patet*. Let me translate: the world is gaping and opens up like a gaze.

Slender-legged tree frog and Boeseman tree frog in the fold of a leaf in French Guiana.

A myriad eyes

Of course, not all things see as I see; even my neighbor is different from me in that respect. They each see things in their own way. From the original unicellular organisms to the most evolved animals, divergent visions succeed each other, as numerous as the generations that can be counted by specialists in this ocular genesis. All things are receptive to light and the information it carries, and so they receive my light and I receive theirs. They all have their own world and each of them is different.

The birth of the eye was not a miracle, but occurred in an innumerable series of generations of photosensitive organs, whose tissues have evolved by the millions since the Cambrian age. They all stem from one molecule, the opsin that captures light and functions as the first and principal selective power, at least on our planet. Two thirds of all animals have analogous organs while plants owe their birth and development to similar cells. Being-in-the-world and clear-sighted, I am seen by countless gazes, by such crazily disparate performances and their infinite kaleidoscope that I dream of seeing them all transmute my pages into brilliant multitudes. I know however I will never see that.

The universe is studded with eyes. Look here.

Behind the eye drawn by Leonardo da Vinci only an empty white space opens up. The encephalon is still reduced to a black box. Anatomy had started to itemize organs but had not yet identified the functions noted by physiology. The eye exists, but not the gaze.

Leonardo da Vinci, *Anatomical Chart of Man*, end of the 16th century, Windsor Royal Library, Windsor Palace.

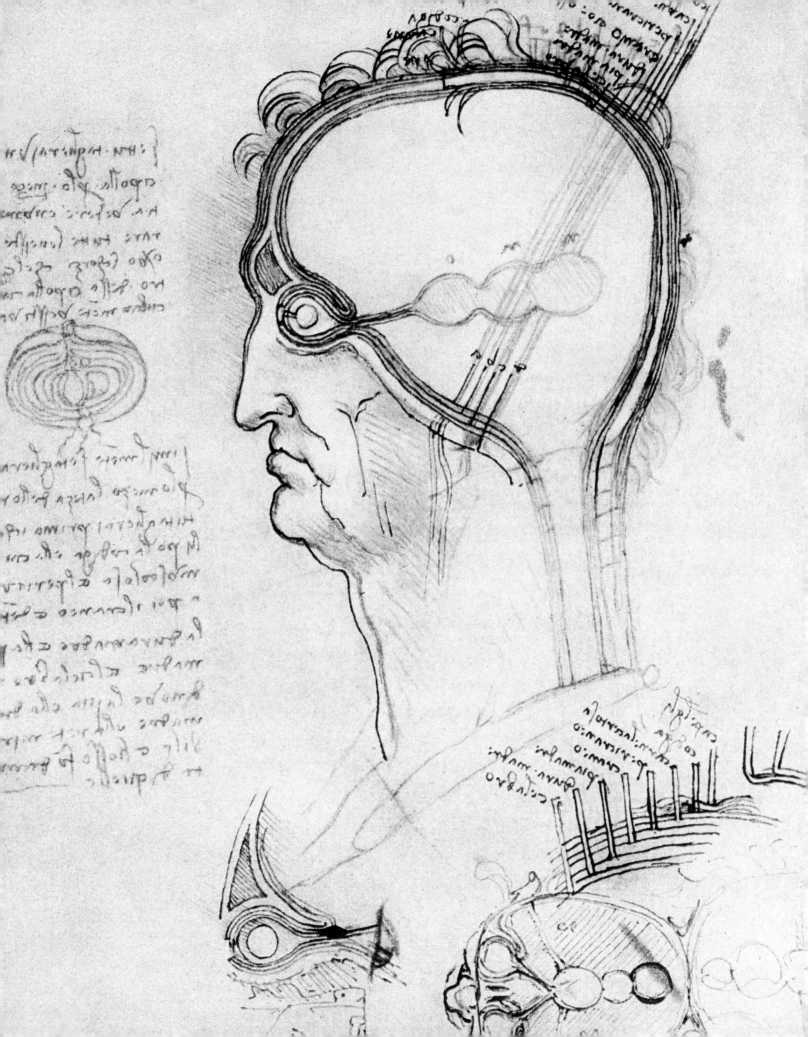

The cave streaming with light

"The two heroes, dazzled by their sudden return to daylight, faced a spectacle which was both so splendid and unexpected, that at first they thought they were the victims of some ecstatic hallucination. Both found themselves in the center of an immense cave. The ground was covered with fine gold-sequined sand. The vault which was as high a Gothic cathedral's, disappeared into unfathomable depths that were impossible to penetrate. The walls of this natural underground structure were covered with stalactites of incredible varied shades and richness, on which the reflections of the torches threw rainbow-colored flames, mixed with fiery blazes and aurora borealis rays [...]

"Rocks of amethyst, onyx, ice fields of rubies, emerald needles, colonnades of sapphires what were deep and tall like pine forests; aquamarine icebergs, girandoles of turquoises, opal mirrors, outcroppings of pink gypsum and lapis-lazuli with gold veins: all that was most precious, rare, limpid and brilliant which the crystalline reign could offer, had been used as materials for this surprising architecture [...] Further on, an artificial lake formed by a diamond of twenty meters set in the sand looked like an arena ready for the frolics of skaters. Overhead palaces of chalcedony, kiosks and pinnacles of beryl and topazes piled up floor after floor, so much so that the eye tired out by all that splendor refused to look at them any longer. Finally, the shattering of the light rays into thousands of prisms, the fireworks of sparkles that exploded everywhere and fell back in sprays, constituted the most surprising symphony in light and color that would dazzle the human gaze."
Jules Verne, *L'Étoile du Sud*, chap. XIX, « La grotte merveilleuse »,
J. Hetzel et Cie, 1884, p. 267-269.

Verne's cavern is the opposite of Plato's cave where he confines his deluded prisoners. His cave sings the glory of one single sun which the freed prisoners discover when, once liberated, they leave the shadows. Verne's new cave invites free people to move under such a deep vault that they can get as lost as when gazing at a starry firmament. Here are thousands of nocturnal sparkles as if the stones were illuminated and looked at each other.

Oysters, geodes, the starry sky: everywhere in the world you will find caverns streaming with light. Open up three black boxes: a simple stone, grain of sand or galaxy but also a word and its meaningful treasures, an emotion-laden secret, an intuition full of ideas, a complex work, a declaration of love promising joy...

Gyrolite with okenite and calcite, Poona, Maharastra, India, coll. UPMC-the Sorbonne.

Sweet night

Philosophers like light, especially the sun's daily brilliance, and treat it as the best model of knowledge. It makes it possible to see. Overflowing with truth, so they say, it chases away the darkness of obscurantism whose active shadows devour clarity. This is absurd and contrary to experience because any candle, no matter how little light it gives, pushes back any nearby shadows, but no one has ever seen darkness defeat light.

On the other hand, if one makes daylight the champion of knowledge, there is only one single totalitarian truth, as harsh and unsubtle as the sun at noon, the star which astrophysics finally relegated to the minor rank of a yellow dwarf. Such ideology is terrifying. No to this tyranny! No to yellow dwarfs!

Daylight gives the illusion that there is only one unique truth. In reality, thought resembles it far less than the night where each star shines like a diamond, where each galaxy streams like a river of pearls, where every planet is like a mirror that returns the glow it receives in its own way. Real knowledge brims over with a million results and insights. It installs many reference points grouped in constellations with forms as different as those of scholarly disciplines. It finds temporary truths whose luxuriously colored brilliance flickers and falters as the Big Story. New stars will also die, like this or that genius' proofs or laboratory's successful experiments. The only lights that do not tremble come from planets without their own original glow which behave mimetically like mirrors. The blue super giants, Vega and Rigel, or a star like the medusa-shaped Antares, are magnificent but sufficiently modest to be reduced to dots. Their size is formidable, but they also shimmer with questions and doubt. These truth-stars come out of the enormous black background of non-knowledge, limitless emptiness, or galaxies that are still inaccessible: there are things to know and understand tomorrow here.

From local astronomy dealing with celestial mechanics to astrophysics, our knowledge has expanded from the world to the universe. The new vision of things and their historical narrative makes us into a different kind of being-in-the-world.

Galaxies UGC 1810 and UGC 1813 of the Andromeda constellation photographed by the *Hubble* telescope in December 2010.

People with night vision

The gap between day and night measures the distance between cruel ideology and real knowledge that is multiple, progressive and controlled, historical and contingent. Shimmering with billions of glorious and timid colored suns, night resembles Verne's cavern with its dazzling gems and innumerable truths linked together by a thousand related networks. This is where thought sparkles, as softly as flowing pearls. More visible and beautiful than the day and peaceful in any case, the night knows while the day pronounces. Stars shiver as they look while the sun's formidable lucidity blinds us.

Fortunately, physiologists confirm my philosophical intuition. By diminishing the electrical signals emitted by nerve cells, light, they tell us, has only an inhibiting effect. What's more, obscurity activates the retina whose cells then emit trains of potential action. Light, however, provokes the hyper-polarization of cones, rods and photoreceptors. Useful information emanates from the difference in lighting. To construct its interpretation of the world, the brain needs contrasting light. For example, when the sun goes down, the rattlesnake gradually sees visible radiations less clearly but infrared better, which allows it to see its prey detaching itself from a cold and obscure background.

Like any hunting animal, knowledge has night vision.

We move toward the intuition of this book. Here we finally see how we see. You see before you closely-packed parallel stalks as they are really seen. They are like a thick bundle of sheaves in a wheat or grass field; in short, they are real, multiple, tangible, solid, mobile, living and yes, visible things. Be careful, these things see, and even better still, without them, who could see?

Retina cells seen under an electronic microscope of the SEM type.

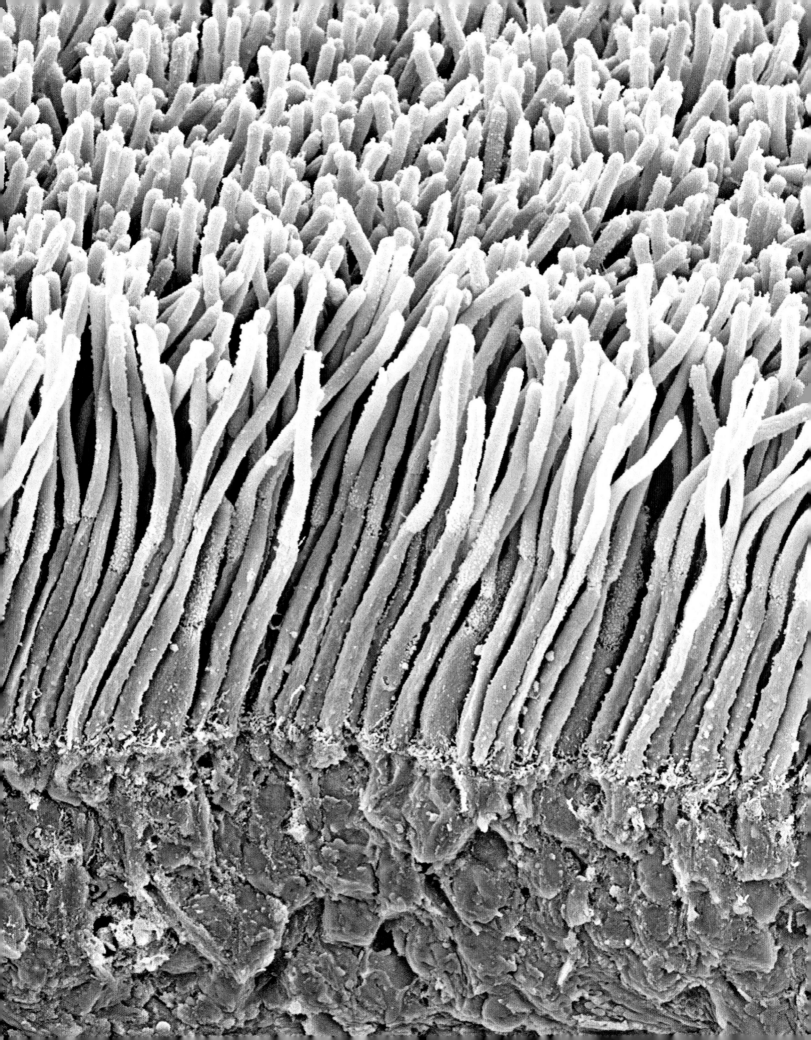

Even worse. To the platonic ideology of a single solar truth, Immanuel Kant added such a narcissistic image that it should have worried wiser men. At a time when the sun was in the center of the world, he

From revolutions

made a sun into the subject of knowledge, in one word, the I-Sun. Today everything should make us laugh at

that turn around

a form of paranoia whose immodest presumption places us on a monarch's throne. We say no to the dwarf who

themselves to an

thinks he is the tyrant of knowledge, especially since the Sun produces light while our eyes only receive it. Whether

expanding Universe

Ptolemaic or Copernican, revolutions that ineffectually turn around a fixed terrestrial or solar point, seem to us

rather localised today.

Astrophysics introduced us to thousands of billions of galaxies that are dense with constellations, black holes and other strange things that color a diverse universe full of scattered Verne-like gems. They are sometimes visible at night. To use Kant for my own purpose here, those suns more or less know and see. There are no more centers everywhere that are more or less attractive: there is no longer one single reference for truth, or the exclusive uniqueness of the subject. There are more or less thoughtful subjects everywhere; there are more or less profound truths everywhere that sparkle in the black background of contemporary blindness and ignorance.

The sky does not only show light points in the darkness of the night, but also intermediary glows whose shades the Ancients compared to those of the milk flowing from a goddess's breasts. This maternal legend gave rise to the term *galaxy*. The limpid grey-white outlook, with grainy dots, is organized into avenues, poles, oval spots, spirals as if chaos were moving forward to some order.

How can we not compare these arrangements in the Universe to the chronic trial and error of our sciences? They invariably develop around attractive ideas and then disintegrate to form around different ideas elsewhere, a movement that is outlined on the dark background of not-knowing.

Galaxy in spiral form Messier 74, or NGC 628, at a distance of 32 million light-years from the Earth.

Matter and mirror

Moreover, Verne's cavern turns Plato's cave upside down by
becoming the small-scale model of the exterior world which, at least
here, is composed of hard material crystals such as corindons or beryls, and
also brilliant mirrors with blazing sparkling light, fireworks with luminous colors.
Multiplying their effects, they emit, receive, exchange, store and deal with countless
data about themselves and others. Do they see as they can be seen? Both material support
and message, diamonds refer back to lapis-lazuli, themselves support and message. Brilliant
sards and rubies echo the blazing aquamarines while emeralds are reflected in huge mirrors of
topazes. Countless substances exchange information and accomplish countless reciprocal metamorphoses. Gems inform each other and in a way converse just like living things including us.
Reversing both the Kant-like Copernican determination and Plato's ancient cave, this cavern shows the
reality of a world that, like the network of a labyrinth, is composed of supports and messages, of mirrors
and rays, of things and thoughts, of matter and information, of hard and soft. Does that brightness sweeping
through and shaping space show that the world's things have their own vision of the world's things, as does
each of us? Yes, these things are seen, but do they also see? They each can become the subject of the objects
they reflect. Verne's cavern shows the vision that the universe has of itself.
The two heroes who went inside, just as precious as those stones and their reflections, are they too changed
into diamonds? They see the gems. Are they seen by their countless eyes?
One should be able to follow the alternating trajectories of those light rays and to calculate how much
information they carry, to tell what they are and sketch how they do it. If I were able to do this, I would
understand the world like the Stoics, Pascal or Leibniz. For them all things, caused, causing, emitting,
and receiving, all agree with each other and conspire together. The beauty of the universe is born from
this harmony.

Hubert Robert painted the ruins of the Louvre invaded by flocks of sheep. Banality enters art, just as light needs darkness.
This image mimicked vision. Here the eye slides over the black walls towards the opening in the back.

Hubert Robert, *The Grotto of Posillipo*, 1769, The Cleveland Museum of Art.

The primitive scene:
the origins of representation

It occurred to me that in spite of its flat story and dull lesson, Plato's old allegory has been imprinted in people's memory for so long because it described an authentically original scene turned upside down. I imagine it goes back like a recollection of immemorial times when our ancestors, those so-called cavemen, who unlike Plato's prisoners, would simply be sitting around the fire. Seeing the dancing shadows of people or animals on the walls around the hearth at the whim of the brilliant fire, they would seize a branch darkened by the flames in order to fix traces of moving profiles. These would   not yet be distinct shapes but the moving dance of shadows and flames. Far from intending to copy "nature", then or now or ever, their actions aimed at understanding its ways and its unfolding laws – *natura*, that which will be born –   and to discern its processes. This was   the beginning of painting and writing   – with a brush or perpetually moving   stylus – and all the representational   arts... even geometry. An analogous   legend, probably just as primitive, tells how   Thales came to the foot of the pyramids   in the noon sunlight and saw his intercept   theorem clearly outlined when he compared the shadow of his body to the building's shadow. In a cavern or before a tomb of   kings, one of the world's things acts   like a   subject, and makes the first move of   invention;   by imitating, we make the second. Active, mobile,   powerful, and   evolving, the fire in the cavern, or the sun at the foot of the pyramids, are both   writing: fire writes an animal's silhouette on the stone wall and the sun writes the   building's triangle. They write: why wouldn't we write too? They paint, we   paint; they represent, we enter the realm of representation. They measure and we   measure.

We act like the world. The world taught us to write, read, paint and represent by writing, reading, painting and representing. Does the world see?

Come in, I said. Brought to tears and astonished by their power of invention, we discovered the masterpieces of Lascaux, with the images or points, and the animals or abstractions. As we looked, the platonic scene recovered its obvious original meaning. Let us now praise those so-called prisoners and inhabitants of the cavern. Here are the geniuses who invented the arts and representational techniques. As for the prisoners who are now free, see how they walk around outside, illiterates without writing, idiots without painting.

They are inattentive outside the cavern, and fail to see objects or bodies in three dimensions, as they really are. Don't you see that in the open air, inside and everywhere, everyone perceives only appearances, sideways or in profile? The above-mentioned immobile prisoners observe and contemplate them and yes, they read those images projected on the slightly uneven or almost level wall in the dark cave. What advanced power of abstraction compared with the fugitive and banal impressions of daylight!

Glory to this primitive scene where reading was invented!

Glory to this primitive scene where painting was invented!

The shadow of something in profile projected by the light of a flame mimics the various traces left by the world's objects on other things. Here we have in reverse, the real lesson of the cavern in question.

Don't leave, go inside!

We enter this cavern all the time

It gets better. Suppose that at each progressive invention in the techniques of representation, we enter some new cavern, then contemporary history would confirm the hypothesis of the Verne-like reversal of Plato's primitive scene. Here it is.

In the work of Piero or Masaccio, who discovered perspective, we admire the floor pavements and the skies of the ceilings with their orderly clouds. We enter theatres. They invent boxes in which they draw points and lines. Let us

hasten to Urbino to walk around *The Ideal City*, which again lies between a low firmament and a uniform podium. For all I know, the dark room or *camera obscura*, the optical instrument which projects light onto a flat space, may reproduce blindly the picture of the old cavern in painting and later in photography. These are not prisoners, but good painters.

The ideal city is often regarded as a utopia. But which urban planner works on his drawing board or in front of his screen without dreaming of creating a harmonious space where his contemporaries could happily spend their lives in peace? Without such a vision, you cannot be an architect.

Luciano Laurana (attributed to), *The Ideal City*, detail, 1460-1470, Galleria nazionale delle Marche, the ducal palace in Urbino.

The classroom with its blackboard has become the indispensable place to learn reading and writing. They are students, not prisoners. When we finally go to see an exhibit at the museum, we enter Plato's cave again. Aesthetes, not prisoners. I still see the photographer look at me through his lens, his head buried under the black cloth. An artist, not a prisoner. What is more, photography certainly made it possible for any individual to exhibit his portrait in public, while in the past, only the grandees of this world could aspire to such publicity by having their portrait painted. Prisoners? Of course not: they are finally on their way to democracy! Even better, we sit down in a movie theatre to follow the story through moving images. Esthetes, not prisoners. I remember that as a child in Montaigu-de-Quercy (Tarn-et-Garonne) I went into a tent in the village center and, in this new cavern for the first time, I was dazzled. I left behind the plow and the soil for Chaplin's America and thanks to Méliès, even the moon! A prisoner? On the contrary, I was liberated and rose up like a rocket without gravitation. On the contrary, I was finally a traveler and citizen of the world.

We pay another visit to ancient celestial mechanics: the Moon and the shell have round, smooth, geometric outlines, drawn by a formally trained mind.
These are the "views" of our old reason.

Jules Verne, *From the Earth to the Moon*, 1877; private collection.

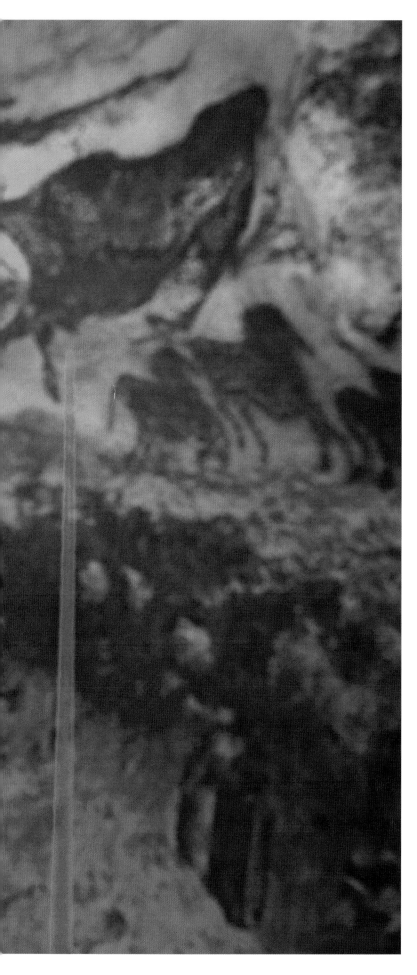

The Lascaux caves

Half a century later, scholarly friends of mine invited me to return to Lascaux but through a virtual door. At *Dassault Systèmes*, a company specializing in graphics, computer simulation and the design of the most sophisticated industrial projects, engineers took me to a laboratory grotto and asked me to put on felt shoes and special glasses. The visitor experiences a mild vertigo as he goes through the walls and flies towards the vault instead of walking like a mortal who is hampered by solid matter. Enchanted to see again the sanctuary that had delighted him in his childhood, he now understands that Plato's cave, far from criticizing the prisoners, on the contrary celebrates the inventors of writing, of painting and representation. He himself has returned to the original place of discovery at the present time when other ways of seeing are invented: when seeing changes, one revisits the origins of vision. A prisoner? You must be kidding! A technician rather among engineers and scholars! In any case, this is someone who ceaselessly repeats the same initial gesture.

There is a short-circuit between the most archaic representations such as the Lascaux caves and digital technology. As our ancestors entered the cave, I go into the laboratory. Which spectacles did the hunter-gatherer painter put on to invent the marvelous new world painted here on the walls? Our own world seems cut off from his by thousands centuries and thousands of ideas. However, his drawings seem so familiar to us that they connect us with the older brother who created *Homo Virtualis*, our real species name. We are indeed virtual in most of our actions, artistic and technical of course, but also in our daily intimate actions.

Photo of Michel Serres visiting the Lascaux cave in 3D at Dassault Systèmes.

Be brave once more: let us go into the dark to see better! Let us go out at night and revisit the cavern that Verne studded with corindon and beryl.

He who encounters Pierre Soulages, soon realizes that he went back to the encyclopedic knowledge of the Renaissance painters, to the humanities and natural sciences, techniques and crafts, culture and the arts; he knows everything. How then could his work not have discovered the excellent model of contemporary knowledge, the sparkling night and luminous darkness?

Exhibit of Pierre Soulages, Rodez, 2014.

stone

eyes

Dredging ecstasy

The tinkling chain joggles on its axis, pulling heavy loads of sand and gravel and pissing water through all its holes. At the top, each bucket empties its load in a trommel whose slow rotation separates large and small grains as they fall noisily in various vats in the barge, which is moored to the port. After each foray on the segment of the river to be dredged, the load emerges again from the good waters of the Garonne, filled to the brim before plunging again into the riverbed, overturned and empty. The dredger and his apprentice are busy with the winches and the motor. The whole platform vibrates and trembles from the giant effort needed to dig vertically into the bottom of the riverbed.

Who sees this stone? I see it going up towards me in its bucket along the chain. No one has seen it; no one except me sees it and no one will ever see it. It passes slowly and on the ground, will fall from the crane into the hopper and then into the crusher to multiply, be ground, fractured into hundreds of pieces of gravel and later mixed in melted asphalt, which solidifies into the surface of a highway. It is lost, forgotten, anonymous and worthless. However, at this moment, in the fraction of this fleeting second, it glistens with a green-yellow polish and the soft and smooth humidity of bluish-green seaweed. Hemispherical and discreet, it shines in a bed of grey gravel like a jewel in a well-designed ornament. I know it will never become a cornaline, a sapphire or an aquamarine and will forever remain ordinary, but here at this moment, it plays its small role wonderfully as a large stone. From the encounter of water and oblivion at the bottom of the riverbed, it is transported from the Pyrenees and rising gently up to the sky, it emerges polished and softened by years of abrasion. It looks at me, mute among the roar of the wind and steel, streaming with tears. Yes, I recognize you as you stare at me as with the river's bulging eyes. The flash of its humble and mystical look is like the spark of the river's pupil pierced by ocelli with their myriads of eyelids.
I am saved. The Garonne has seen me.

When the author of this book built his own house, he erected a wall whose façade he could see from the house, similar to the one here, so he could keep near him the stones of the Garonne, more precious in his eyes than the diamonds of Golconda.

Wall of the Catalan bridge, built with pebbles from the Garonne.

Eyes of corindon and beryl

River pebbles are the proletarians; the semi-precious stones such as aquamarines or turquoises are the bourgeois; diamonds and rubies are princes and marquesses; gems and pearls, baronesses and duchesses. My book throws a revolutionary look on this classification.

Rhodochrosite, N'Chwaning, Kuruman, Northern Cape, South Africa, col. UPMC-the Sorbonne.

One day I had a wonderful opportunity to work with a master jeweller in the center of a big city. This wise man invited me to visit the workshops where designers and draftsmen were making diamond necklaces, brooches, bracelets and pendants. He put a few exquisite gems such as emeralds, diamonds, sapphires and rubies in my hand. Did my palm become more valuable?

My eyes on those mirrors, those sources of light looking into each other's eyes, I reminded my host of the device

of Thumbelina, who with her cell phone in her hand, can visit any corner of the world with GPS, obtain any information through Wikipedia and finally reach anyone in the world with a few phone calls. Thumbelina can now say: "Now I hold the world in my hand." She is talking about the miraculous and versatile object from which any available information, all virtual possibilities can emerge. She can utter the phrase which none of history's most powerful crowned heads could have pronounced.

Holding those stones in my hand I was thinking that like the girl with the cell phone I was holding the world in my hand because they contained all possible colors, from milky to intense hues, from the red of currants to the purple of prunes, in other words a complete rainbow spectrum. The world itself is studded with such precious stones as well as stones we value less, and ceaselessly exchanges its own light. It reflects back all information from anywhere towards any place, to its own eyes. I can leave, Thumbelina can disappear, but even in the absence of any subject, all the world's objects know how to emit, store, receive and handle information, things that she and I thought could only be said and done by us. That day I understood that the world was not what I was told, a passive entity, but instead that our being-in-the-world lived and thought in Verne's lucid cavern.

The world looks at itself. Is it also looking at us?

Phidias and Titian were not the only ones
to dream of the shape of the female body.
Not only Degas and Rodin, not only
you and I, day and night, but all humanity
since its dawn.

Feminine statuette in polished stone,
middle Neolithic, national museum of
Archeology in Saint Germain-en-Laye.

All the world's stones

Indeed, the world looks at us. This is how.
At the beginning of my book, I celebrated paintings whose brilliance
and sensitivity seemed to make us forget the grey canvas underneath.
Someone, for instance, who deciphers traces left by animal
paws, often forgets the stones and mud on the ground.
We ignore the earthen or stone support while
silently we read the mark's message because it
speaks to us. We call anyone who can see the
canvas beneath the image subtle.
As I have said many times, in the age of oral
communication, the support-message couple
at transmission appeared as sound waves
coming from the transmitting body and as
voices perceived by the listening body when
received. Support-messages equalled body-
waves. Language had not yet left music behind.
When writing emerged, the message changed from heard
or transmitted sound waves, to an alphabet carved by hand and
perceived by eyes. The support left the body and became a wall or a rock, or
a stone barrier, a marble stele, a wax tablet, calf skin, velum, sheepskin, parchment
and finally paper, *biblos*... and soon thereafter the infinitely thin geometer's drawing. These
have become the underlying support, almost hidden and less visible. The transfer from body
as support to the infinitely flat drawing at once unites the origins of geometry and writing and
possibly of painting as well, in short all representation. How did a warped or flat material
support emerge and receive information?
Whether we paint, carve, write, draw or calculate, either on a piece of bronze or a marble
slab, an animal hide, a roll, a coin, a canvas, a page, a wall with graffiti, a computer,
or cell phone screen, it is still the same more or less flat support. No other has
ever been invented. We are back at the soil with traces moulding footsteps
and stone as well as the carved stele. In other words, the message varies
in its content and form, in time and space, while the flat surface
remains almost universal. Diverse, changeable and floating,
writing itself is not in question: the deeper problem
concerns the support.

From the figure to the sign

How am I to understand the connection between the message and the support, what "knowing how to read" means or even "knowing how to see"? Let us go back to the animal tracks seen in stone or mud. In his *Neurones de l'écriture*, Stanislas Dehaene asks the question of the origin: "What was the use of those neuronal powers we employ for reading today, before writing was invented, before anyone could have read any message on any kind of support?" The author imagines that the ancestors of those printed marks were precisely the traces left by game on the soil. Any experienced hunter will recognize the tracks of a stag, boar or partridge, as well as its age, sex, health condition or pregnancy, and the precise moment of its passage. In fact, he reads a kind of proto-writing. All this information amounts to a projection, in the geometric sense of the term.

How can we describe this projection? Did you see below the figures in Lascaux the long series of dots that today's technologies are able to combine into a virtual figure? The minute details of the traces refer to the larger units of bodies or behaviours, as if inversely, the large concrete features of size, sex and feathers could be summarized or condensed, and were literally projected, feature by feature, into those details engraved in stone or mud. And so we have a quasi-abstract portrait! The subject is thrown into this projection, summarized in a number of objective signs.

Projections

Significantly, the last sentence outlines a specifically cognitive link between the subject, thrown under – *sub-jectus* – and the object, thrown in front of – *ob-jectus* –, this link being precisely a forward projection, *pro-jecta*. All philosophy of representation, even its origin and essence, is contained in those three words and even more so in their common verb, to throw.

Let us look at the trajectory of rays. Flames in the fireplace and sunrays transport, transmit and throw the animal's profile onto the stony wall of the cave as in Plato's myth, or the pyramids' triangle on the desert sand in the story of Thales' adventure. In Verne's cavern, sard and aquamarine throw their radiance onto the hard brilliant surface of the rink. The galloping sow sculpts, throws and leaves behind traces of its four paws in the mud. The young boars with smaller feet leave as many traces and marks as their mother. Generally speaking, would there be a prehistory without those traces preserving on stone what was thrown there? Like gems, things of the world today throw their glimmer on each other. They show themselves and become readable.

Great artists are often said to have left their mark on history. This is also said of tyrants and strategists, and killers. Wolves, lions and rabbits have done the same on the peaceful earth since the dawn of the living. However, rain on dust, the wind on the seas and the rivers in the valleys also hollow out their own original marks.

Traces of a hare's paws in the snow.

The good hunter who bends over to examine animal tracks can guess the age, sex, the whole body and even the present behavior of the stag or sow who just ran past. Now infer the Spring Venus from her toe.

Sandro Botticelli, *The Birth of Venus*, c. 1485, Galleria degli Uffizi, Florence.

Traces of footsteps

After writing and reading, comes painting. The neuronal and hunting hypothesis, and the evocation of hunters gatherers' paintings on the walls of Lascaux, is reminiscent of the crazy image described by Balzac in *The Unknown Masterpiece*. On the painter's canvas, amidst a messy chaos of forms and colors, among a lot of sound and fury, the mark of a magnificent foot appears. As a projection, it designates a beautiful creature from the sea, emerging from the background noise like Venus emerging from the waves. You could read that footprint as Botticelli's *Aphrodite*, standing up straight, flattened as a planar projection. The substance of all beauty is projected on that footprint.

But be careful. This foot is not a foot, but the stone pressed by the volume and weight of Aphrodite's body. It is a stone, no, it is not a stone but the foot of the passing animal whose weight and volume carved it. Visible and legible, those traces designate – without however opening it – the black box that contains the secret and mystery of the alliance between stone and sign, matter and form, hardware and software, hard and soft. In spite of the absence of any documentation of this prehistory, I think that Dehaene is right. In the vision of those traces of the hunt or perhaps divine traces, lies the origin of reading, writing and all forms of representation, including painting.

Moreover, our classical authors used the term "perspectival representation" to designate the profiles under which any object appears seen from a thousand points of view. Can we conceive of the sum of all those profiles, they asked? Only an omnipresent God, who sees every point of view, could contemplate this integral. They called it geometral but also an ichnographic. The word ιχνοσ in classical Greek designates the trace of a step, a footprint!

After painting, the proof. Among the first Greek geometers, the Euclidian plane, which was either the first or exquisite support, is called επιπεδου, *epipedon*. Concretely, this term signifies "on ground level". Abstractly, it means united like a geometric drawing, that is, a geometry that soon will be perspectival or projective!

A thousand traces of passing

The preceding pages went from drawings or full-length portraits to the traces left on stone or the soil, from the figurative to the abstract. This passage is made by footsteps or imprints.

This concerns not only Aphrodite's body or the hunt, or writing and reading. Along the banks of the Garonne river, the passage of slow or turbulent waters has discharged heaps of small rounded stones into curved gravel. On the shores of Brittany, the tides' movements leave or throw up peaks and capes of lacy pink or emerald granite. Winds from the Sahara desert deposit red particles on glaciers in the Alps. The boring of icecaps allows us to see the flows of dust scattered here and there and so enables us to read the climate's millenary history. Volcanic rocks in Auvergne keep traces of the magnetic field inserted when they crystallized. Many stones conserve fossils that allow us to reconstitute the fauna and flora of past times. Thanks to carbon 14, we can date a lot of things. And so there are footprints all over the world and we find traces of passages, of everything that happened in the past. Almost every period projected its passage. And so the world manifests itself.

This is no longer just about writing and reading or painting and representation. We are dealing now with all those sciences that today read and date things, inviting us to consider the things of the world as supports for words and material, but also as signs engraved on stones. The world invites us to enter Verne's cavern, encrusted with gems, corindons and beryls, scintillating like eyes, gems exchanging their luminous rays.

All our sciences show that the world is full of matter and information everywhere, linked like an inseparable couple. Everywhere support and projection marry. There are footprints on stone and ocelli everywhere.

Narcissus is said to look at himself in the water. Under their arches, bridges are reflected there so calmly that the original and its image form one oval mirror.

Reflection under a bridge in France.

sea
eyes

Sea and land ocelli

Old marine maps, decorated with fish and small figures, are often oriented with thorny compass roses. The history of these marine maps shows the progressive arrival of the sciences in the art of navigation through which empirical perception can be eliminated little by little. I remember fishing vessels that did not use maps in the 1950s. Accustomed to the deep sea waters between Fécamp and Saint John's, they were just as comfortable there as Parisians in the metro or as the villagers who pass without thinking through the neighbor's vineyard to the cemetery behind the church. Those fishermen saw the sea that my sextant and my logging tables prevented me from observing. I calculated angles and numbers while they saw colors change, currents forming, cetaceans blow while they sniffed out where the wind was going. Calmly, they crossed the multi-colored surface, that is, a legible map right on a sea that itself had plenty of eyes. The marine map was not on paper but spread out before them, fluctuating among the waves. I thought I was a scholar and considered them empirical. We would arrive together in Iceland or Labrador.

Something happened that took me and my fisher friends out of circulation. The use of a sextant forces the sailor to know the deepest corners of the sky since he often has only one precious minute in which to take a bearing when the sun goes down and the horizon is still visible and the first star is lit. It can still shine in the clouds whose mass hides all the other stars. This means that one needs to know its name, brilliance, color and particular shine. I was going to say that scintillating, it winked at us. We were reading the night sky like a familiar page on which the constellations traced a range of notes where each star sounded one; on which they showed the paths where each star left a mile-stone; and on which they exhibited their peacock tail studded with ocelli. We inhabited this vault, a village actually, a metropolis where we users circulated like the above-mentioned villager in the avenue or the Parisian at the Châtelet. I saw the sky like my fisherman saw the sea. He inhabited the ocean while I haunted the firmament that changed according to the seasons, latitudes, hemisphere, climate, storm and calm before the storm. The two of us both inhabited the view. He could hesitate while I calculated my errors. We arrived together in Iceland, his eyes fixed on the waves, and mine on the viewfinder of the sextant. However, holding the log and the sky map in my hand, I felt superior because of my knowledge of angles and numbers and thought my fisherman was stuck in empirical reality. Then we were both out of it. With techniques whose refinement elicits my admiration, the GPS swept me and the old sea dog away sending us together to the historical open-hopper dredge. Off to the scrap heap! Now the sea and sky are no longer our homes; the era of sight is shut off, and our two common empiricisms have become gar- bage. Crossing space with electronic speed, signals that travel between a satellite and a vehicle, ship, car, or pedestrian, now suffice to determine any position by drawing a map of the site. Blindly, we now know where we are and where we are going. The map is drawn as we travel through space. Even better, sometimes a voice advises us gently to turn right or left and finally tells us, "Welcome, you have arrived!" We have become Tobiases and we hear the archangel Raphael chatting on board.

The rest of us poor fishermen have become aware that one of those two perceptual quasi-maps resided in the waters below, while the other was in the sky, very high up. We sailed by sight by following the eyes of the world, those of the wavelets or those of the constellations. Just as my astronomical positioning and its calculating map relegated the fisherman to the merely qualitative view, the precision of a GPS pushed me towards the completely approximate. This is the hard but just law: every emerging science rejects the preceding one as merely sensory. I became the visual twin of the fisherman, his empiricist brother. The progressive disappearance of the landscape transferred the maps of the sea and the sky to the screen. The byte got the better of the pixel.

Nevertheless, I still haunt my vaulted home, my old cave, and I remain an inhabitant of the sky.

Those Nereids straddling dolphins, the squadrons of royal galleys with their sails, the giant shells that became treasures, the compass roses with their hundreds of petals, the seals with family crests: all these show that marine maps still hesitated between painting and the geographic map when heraldry filled half the space. They display not so much earth and water as mythology, power and glory. This map, which is more a painting than a route chart, is full of trifles that are useless for navigation.

Augustin Roussin, *Portulan de l'Atlantique: Europe de l'Ouest et Afrique du Nord*, aquarelle on paper, 1630, municipal library of Marseille.

MER OCCEANE

J. de Bracilli

Carte
de la Mer
Oceane

FRANCE

57

Fires and foggy signals

The lifted arm, the higher wave around the drowning man, the black spot announcing the grave, the vapors that mix the water from the sky with tears, the three ominous birds...which sailor has ever seen this décor in the worst moments? This is a theatre setting, a tragic shipwreck for landsmen!

Louis Gernery, *The Shipwrecked Man*, c. 1850, Museum of Fine Arts of Brest.

We are following the Côtes-du-Nord several miles off the coast. For greater safety I had found a foothold, because these are bad waters full of sandbanks and other pitfalls. You cannot be too careful. I have midnight watch. It is two in the morning and I am alone on the bridge where two guards are sleeping on either side. I have one eye on the sticky fog, and one eye on the radar screen, and listen intently. A tad anxious, with two hundred sailors sleeping below, I drink more coffee, trying hard not to go to sleep myself. Awake, I was dreaming about my training when the commander on the bridge of a squadron escort ordered me to follow one of the two ships at the horizon straight ahead. I opened my eyes wide but only saw the blue line of the water. After a few weeks at sea, I had bragged about even seeing the quartermaster's cap! Back to reality! The dull graying eye of the empty electronic screen indicates there is no one ahead, the coast is clear; we are traveling at twelve knots, in a middling sea; there is no problem except for that opaque disturbing fog. Suddenly on the screen, there is a small island straight ahead. My bearing is wrong and it has been wrong since I started my watch. At this speed, I cannot stop. In an instant we will smash into the rocks. A river of sweat is streaming down my back, from my neck to my waist. Negligent, I will kill my friends. I am the worst of all sailors, an absolute nothing. And I too will die. The radar's greenish eye charges me with error and crime. This is agony. Torrential rain beats down on my head and I am drenched. I am frozen, drowning but ecstatically happy as I had never been until that night. Suddenly I understood that the radar – which in those remote times was still rudimentary – had intercepted a heavy squall which I had taken for an island.
Saved! My radar's grayish eye returns to his usual calm.

Ocelli, again

Like young fish, we used to swim to the bridge piers downstream where long avenues of large and small turbulent eddies were unfurling, each feeding the other. We laughed at the fury of our parents who thought every day they would see us drown. Like water dervishes, we spun around in those whirlpools that sometimes pulled us to the bottom of the Garonne; however, a sidelong kick on the spongy riverbed propelled us up to reappear far downstream, in the middle of the current. With that training, I could waltz with my sister in the evening on a small table whose only leg was held by my crouching brother.

Panoptic. After the bridge, the river shows its peacock eyes. Pedestrians standing on the bridge deck would see us emerge from those eye-like whirls, the real and often invisible springs whose perpetual tears provide our Garonne river with water. What is the Garonne seeing and why is it weeping?

At the exact moment that high tide gives way to low tide, there is no current, not one eddy below the bridge's curves. The Garonne becomes a lake where the piers are looking at themselves, like Narcissus. Instead of eyes shaped downstream by turbulent spirals, the expanse of water facing the arches and the arches facing the expanse of water, together offer a quiet look.

Stone bridge in Bordeaux.

My childhood flowed through the riverbed and gave me a river man's eye. Since then, I have always loved the Amazon, the Nile, the Yangzi Jiang, the Brahmaputra and the Mississippi, and especially the Saint-Laurent. No river has a laminar flow. Its stream flows down in turbulent avenues. Look at the Loire in Nantes, the Tagus in Lisbon, the Danube in Budapest or in Rumania. All have eye-like eddies that are round like apples fringed with wrinkles and creases. It looks as if they were weaving rugs. What do the rivers see and why are they weeping?

Panoptic. The Universe too is studded with immense peacock tails. Through the eyes of those whirling galaxies, billions of which were created billions of years, even billions of light years ago, it sees itself as a conscious being. Can immanence sometimes look somewhere other than in itself and for itself?

Which misfortune, which happiness is the Universe deploring?

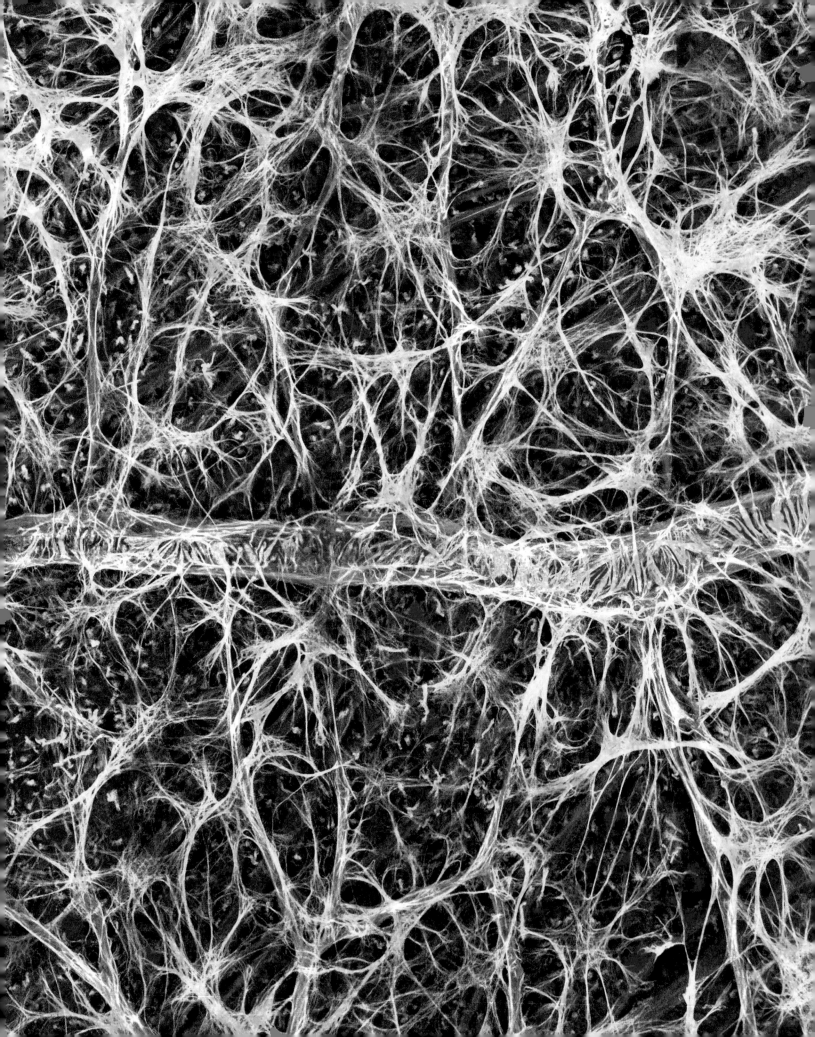

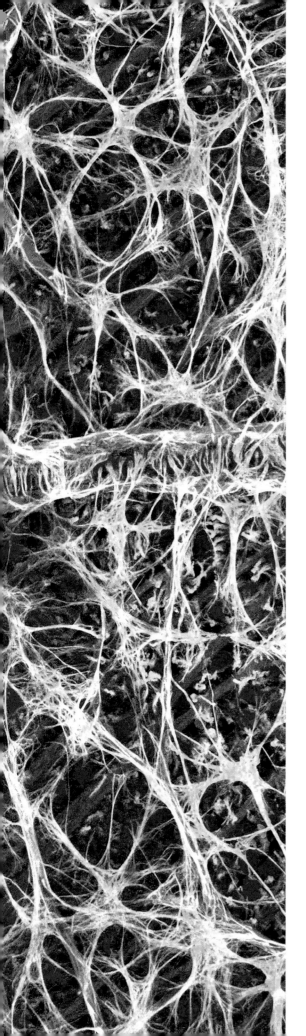

Sea light

Until recently, probably the muslim Middle Ages, our ancestors hesitated to decide whether the eyes of the living, including ourselves, received or emitted light. Optics decided: eye cells are sensitive to light but do not produce any. I respect this correct and if I dare say, evident opinion, but I regret it since I know that certain pupils release clear jets of hate or compassion. The Universe is studded with its own gazes.

Panoptic: when they survive, sailors tell of gigantic or indeed evil waves, an unimaginable wall or a mountain canyon. Until recently, no one believed them. They also sing of the lull after the storm, and of dream-like voyages. The gentlest waters remain between extremes, and show cute wavelets, short-lived ripples as if brilliant, mischievous, and modest Nereids were coming and going, showing and hiding themselves. What or whom are the sea's innumerable smiles so happy about?

On deck of the galley Earth stand billions of masts that the sailor inhabitants call trees. Small sails are attached to their branches that are drawn to light like eyes, moving constantly in the wind. Pushed into its rigging of leaves by winds from different directions, by the Mistral, the Tramontane, the Sirocco and such, the Earth turns on itself.

Excessively calm weather sometimes checks these shifts, slows down its movements. Then storms, hurricanes and cyclones, with angry stares at those delays, rush whirling in to make up for time lost in the lull. And so sails the ship.

Panoptic. A thousand whirlwinds coming from the Mediterranean plunge into the Atlantic to discharge their saltiness.

Panoptic. A thousand whirlpools plunge into the Atlantic to unload their dirt into the deep ocean. Seen from high-up satellites, these turbulences cover air and water, with feathered tails that have eyes. What is the sea looking at and deploring? A thousand successive frothing cyclones emerge from the Gulf of Mexico.

There is nothing more universal than the network format. Everything that exists or knows, both our thoughts and world events, consenting or conspiring, everything just follows the outlines of its ways and connections. Organic systems such as the vision under discussion, function according to this form.

Blood vessels and nerve cells seen under an electronic microscope.

The cyclone

Outward bound for Puerto Rico, insomniac and starving, we remained
hours on end in the Belém airport, waiting for the cyclone to go
north, as the crackling loudspeaker had announced it would.
More adventurous than the others, a skilful pilot decided to
take off, climbing to the highest possible altitude at
cruising speed. We flew over the gigantic circumference
where clouds pressed together, like a bulging shield
around a hole, a center and yes, an empty clear pupil
or a sort of teet or nipple. With my own eyes I saw
this globe whose monstrous eye taunted our aircraft.
As a young midshipman I learned the saving
distinction between the maneuvering half-circle
where the movement of the whirlwind impedes the
direction in which the cyclone is rapidly turning, and
the dangerous half-circle where the two speeds add
up, translation and rotation. In one case, the ship has no
resistance to the wind or waves and will surely be wrecked.
In the other case, it can survive. Everything turns around the
eye. Never lose sight of it...

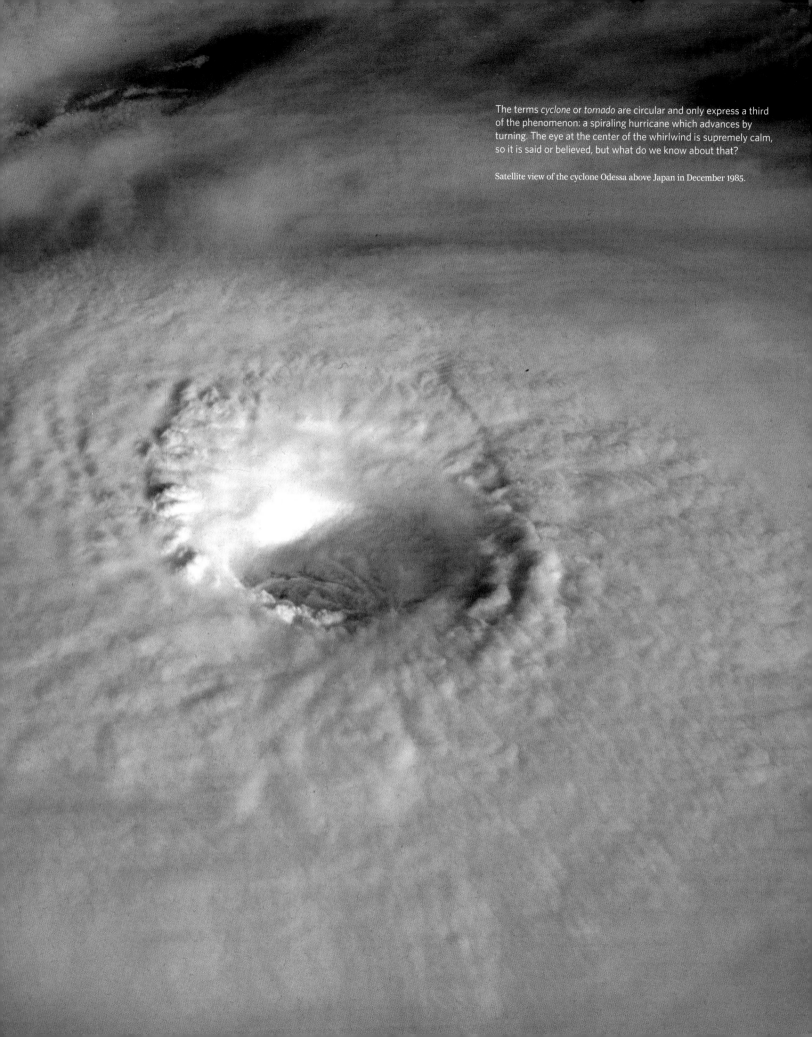

The terms *cyclone* or *tornado* are circular and only express a third of the phenomenon: a spiraling hurricane which advances by turning. The eye at the center of the whirlwind is supremely calm, so it is said or believed, but what do we know about that?

Satellite view of the cyclone Odessa above Japan in December 1985.

The telescopes aboard satellites show the landscapes of outer planets with more details than I knew about the farms in the Lot-et-Garonne when I was a child. Two Earths could hide away in Jupiter's eyes.

Red spot on Jupiter seen from the space probe *Voyager 2*, July 6 1979 (distance: 2.6 million kilometers).

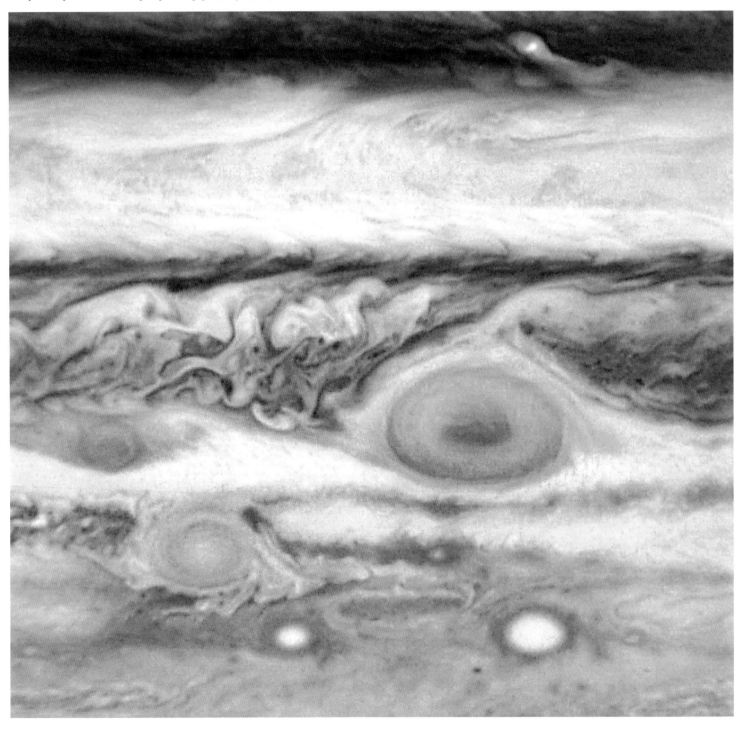

... or of the big red spot called the eye of Jupiter, an oval cyclone 12,000 by 25,000 kilometers, large enough to easily contain two Earths. Does the master of the gods scowl at us from this outer planet? Its powerful attraction protects us from being bombarded with many asteroids and we should call it Polyphemus. A Cyclops cyclone.

Quebec

Let us return to the cycle of the seasons. Give me the name of a land so beautiful that half the year it can compete with the sky. There are rosy, vermillion, crimson tints, Indian Summer reds with their thousand shades, the scarlet display of maples, the thousand and one whites of either bright or brownish-grey snow; in the winter this blessed country sends back to the firmament colors and light so intensely diffracted that the sun itself, from high above, gives the soil only ordinary rays in the summer. Tell me about a country that is more beautiful than its sky, which dazzled, high up, sees what is below fly away in ecstasy and happiness.

Darkness

I like to walk in the dark: inside by feeling for walls or doors, but especially outside, at night, when the moon is veiled and the soles of your feet can make out the road which is harder than the shoulder. I now understand the myth of Argus, that I will celebrate later, telling how and where the panoptic guard was changed into a peacock, whose eyes, called ocelli, are scattered everywhere, not on the skin but on the feathers so that its body perceives obstacles from a distance. I roam around blindly.

During the day we light up rooms, cities, roads and ports. Lamps and tubes take the place of daylight. Although we have become strangers to the shades of sundown and dawn, we still see. Whatever time it is, our clear heads are stuck at noon. No shadow, no night. Seen from an airplane, our Earth is studded with constellations, while on the ground the starry sky disappears, pushed away by the glare of our electric nights. We live like prisoners in a cavern of light. Let us overturn old images: does the search for truth follow the path of shadows?

Nothing is more wrong than John's words: "Light glows in the dark but the shadows did not receive it." As if the shadows had the power to refuse light! On the contrary, darkness is so weak before the smallest glimmer that as soon as the latter appears, darkness flees. Light always conquers while obscurity always beats a retreat. However, I respect and try to protect the lowly darkness which is less peremptory, less arrogant, less harrying than invasive brilliant light. I like shadows, my sister, a fragile beggar who rests my eyes.

While light and pollution hide the night sky, we admire the photos of the constellation formed by England and London, its alpha star, the Benelux constellation and the triple star of its ports, in short, an entire firmament inverted with differentiated sparkles. See this map on Earth as in Heaven.

A satellite view of Western Europe, at night.

Who among us remembers having walked through long corridors, in the dark and cold, holding a flickering candlestick, whose small weak flames, flattened by the breeze of the walk projected obliquely long shadows on the walls? The obscurity was so dense that terrifying creatures had to emerge! We have chased away those familiar phantoms that enriched the imagination.

Even trees can die from illness. We have seen the disappearance of elms, and soon that of sycamore trees. Will chestnut trees, threatened by the plague, perish? Can we imagine an avenue without linden trees, parks without maple trees, fields without oak trees or apple trees, a planet without forests? Can one conceive of a shadowless earth cleaned of those valiant upright bodies and their raised arms that consume white light and project darkness?

Can we think of some truth without a margin of error, without the obscure wavering of the unknown, without a quest's uncertainties, without unexpected innovations, without a *reductio ad absurdum*, without falsifiable experiences? My intuitions twinkle like fireflies in the night I inhabit. I do not know, I grope around. I flounder in the thick manure of ignorance. The face of the true is black and fertile. I think and therefore I live in the night. When you appear, beautiful as a stained-glass window, the dawn softly clears away the eclipse of absence and I emerge from a tunnel.

New inversion: light comes from below while the shadow slides upwards. The fire in the hearth projects a thin silhouette as if it were writing a letter on the wall. We know through spectrums, and not only the stars.

J. H. W. Tischbein *The Great Shadow*, water-colour, c. 1805, Landesmuseum für Kunst und Kulturgeschichte of Oldenburg

glass
eyes

Stained-glass windows

French children learn in school that deep darkness prevailed in the Middle Ages. However, has anything been built since those so-called dark days that is more beautiful, learned, and accomplished than those Romanesque cathedrals in the south and Gothic ones in Bourges, Chartres, Reims and Amiens? Which painter later mixed more splendid colors than in the illuminated manuscripts of the *Très Riches Heures du Duc de Berry?* Which philosopher has been wiser than Francis or more learned than Thomas Aquinas? Please enlighten my own era with that kind of darkness. They even knew how to hide their true colors. Come to a Gothic building. From the outside, the stained-glass window looks greyish, both full and empty, and its hue is the same as that of the even grainier stone. It looks rather plain. However, very creatively, the colored diamond-like glass stones are inserted in a more flexible grid of supports making it almost as resistant as live bone or scales.

Now come inside. The nuclear ocellus tells fabulous fairytales, full of flowery or animal illustrations, multiple canonical stories, popular or mystical characters. They are magenta red in Bourges, spectacularly greenish-blue in Chartres. Lemony, jade-green, yellow and purple light inundates bodies; skins are punctured by a hail of splendid emeralds and pearls, cataracts of garnets, tourmalines and topazes, and showers of sapphires, lapis-lazuli and rubies. All these corindons and beryls of Golconda pierce the skin until they reach the soul that levitates on rainbows.

Seen from the outside, a taciturn woman, a folded kimono, a discreet act, a hidden gift, a sealed letter, a difficult work, a banal holiness, an incredible religion – *Deus Absconditus – [The Hidden God]* all these only speak of simplicity and monotony. However, as soon as you enter the transept, a thousand suns sweep diagonally over the dark shadows now lined with colored rays. Numerous nuclear colors, now completely exposed, explode in the sacred arch studded with ocelli.

In his sleep, Joseph sees more clearly than in a dream his destiny as chaste father and caring foster parent. The humble servant of the Holy Family is absent from the divine genealogy and its representations. Paternity is shelved!

Bourges Cathedral, c. 1210.

Vision works in the following way: there is no space without color; there is no color without space, which is its invariant. In geometry, Pythagoreans called the plane "color." And our globes? Topology demonstrates a theorem of the four colors; we do not need more than that to play cards.

Do you have a dictionary? It classifies words according to the alphabet, *alpha, beta*. The words combine letters, and sentences combine words. This is how you speak and write. Do you play music? You have learned how to read music, *sol, fa*... Well then, now go and sing, play and compose. Do you want to understand the nature of things? They are composed of atoms: oxygen, nitrogen, iron, copper... all classified in the so-called Mendeleyev table of elements. When combined, they form molecules, crystals, rocks, air, clouds, continents, seas and rivers, stars and galaxies. The more elementary genetic code produces paramecium and mushrooms, whales and sequoias, beautiful women and cruel males... With the elements l, m, n, a formidable combinatory in every domain fills the Universe with live beings, enchanting music and languages. Music and language include the world and the living because they are produced in the same mode.

What about colors? There are three additive or subtractive primary colors. Does this produce a table of elements that is as decisive and productive as the preceding ones? The Pantone catalogue shows a table as a range or alphabet with numerous hues, close to eight hundred. This catalogue seems difficult to establish. In the continuous spectrum of possible hues, or if you prefer, in a widely displayed rainbow, a few discrete, that is discontinuous boundaries, need to be chosen to mark the precise tint that can be reproduced, imitated, chosen, ordered and sold. My eyes would be lost assessing them. Does Pantone open our eyes to the facets of an insect where a thousand tints would appear in a thousand colored worlds? I admit I could not draw up such a list but I employ it to educate my vision. I believe everyone has a major sense. The five senses are not distributed homogenously: in some people hearing is privileged, for others, taste, touch, smell or vision. We must train the ones that lag behind.

These dark Middle Ages did not know anything, I tell you. No, geometry was not needed to hew a stone that would fit in a vaulted arch thirty meters high. No, it was better to have no knowledge of chemistry or crystals to cut those stained-glass windows and saturate them with colors that would last for centuries!

Gentle as a purring cat, the lion with its brushed mane, closed jaws, naïve eye, low back, seems to look for a leash rather than terrify those close to him or his prey.

Zosimus and Mary the Egyptian show a Middle Ages without Puritanism, without fear. For three decades, this nymphomaniac woman went from orgy to orgy just for her own pleasure without ever being a prostitute. Zosimus welcomed her and this stained glass window venerates her, as Christ did for the sinner Magdalene.

Bourges Cathedral, c. 1210.

Impressionism: Monet's eyes looked at the lilies in the Giverny pond as if those eye-flowers gazed at him and at us. These stagnant fresh waters organize their panopticon in the Spring.

Claude Monet, *Nymphéas*, 1916, Museum of Western Art, Tokyo.

Is there actually a perfect vision the way we speak of perfect hearing? Do you remember the astronomer who drew the horns of Venus, even though we only discovered them later, with a new telescope? Who saw them in a dark cave where some ancestor had drawn them perhaps millennia before the telescope was invented?

If like me you are just a huge ear, go to Chartres and Bourges to dive into the dawn of stained-glass windows. Look at the jewellery displays and let yourself be pierced by arrows emanating from rubies, emeralds, sapphires and diamonds. Lie down in meadows in the Alps, California, or Tunisia when spring shows a profusion of flowers. Do not miss the apple and apricot trees, or the cherry blossoms in Japan or in the Garonne valley. Look at the bluebirds, red cardinals, and the brilliant eye-shaped spots on peacocks and macaws. And turn the pages of the *Très riches heures du Duc de Berry*; take your time in front of Monet's *Nymphéas,* or their colorful incarnation which the painter saw in the Rouen cathedral.

They will give your eyes plentiful nourishment. I like to use the old word "*ouiller*," to fill up to your eyes, used by wine growers as they refill a vat where the level has gone down through evaporation.

Travel. Our forebears thought more geographically and called the metro line Orleans-Clignancourt or Neuilly-Vincennes. Today we say line 4 or 1. As a foreigner or illiterate, I would take the yellow line, and change via the purple or black line to the red A or the blue B line. Not knowing the alphabet, I would follow the colors.

Can they become an alphabet? Nothing we see is colorless. A formidable explosion of colors must have produced innumerable shades, just as many combinations as the genetic code of the animal species; or the number of atoms for the things in the world; there must have been as many as needed to play or sing musical compositions; as many as the alphabet made to speak and read. Do we understand things as combinations of elements as in the case of music and language? Do we understand and see this when we imitate the world's unique gesture?

Red

Hergé's wife worked in his studio as a colorist [Hergé was the author of the *Tintin* cartoon series]. I owe her a discovery. When she was widowed, she called me one morning to tell me about a new project. On a square in Brussels some people wanted to put Tournesol's moon rocket. They wanted to build it as high as the Eiffel Tower with elevators and restaurants, theatres and shops; in other words, a gigantic building. She asked me to give this design some thought.

Thanks to her, I became conscious of red. When our eyes are at leisure, they may encounter large expanses of blues and greens, such as seas, skies, steppes or tropical forests; or large areas of yellow for instance in ripe wheatfields in the summer. However, have we ever seen such a huge expanse of reds? Could we tolerate this color, in the city or the countryside if it were as widespread as the blue in the sky or the green of the meadows? The rosy-fingered dawn or the copper-colored sunsets don't have those large blood-red squares that adorn Tintin's missile. Could one of the primary colors affect us differently than the two others? I believe it does. Is it the horrifying effect of blood or inversely, the excellence ascribed to it by the Russians or Chinese? In any case, red is different. The missile was never built. Would we ever have been comfortable with its size?

However, one day I saw a large poppy field in Provence. Could my eyes have deceived me?

Austrian symbolism or Art Nouveau in Vienna: Klimt's eyes looked at the poppies as if eye-flowers gazed at him and at us. The wheat or barley harvests organize their panopticon in the Summer.

Gustav Klimt, *Poppy Field*, 1907, Österreichische Galerie Belvedere, Belvedere Palace, Vienna.

La Fontaine is also wrong: this concerned a real astronomer. A very old legend from before Æsop tells how washerwomen, their hands red from beating the clothes, mocked and laughed at the scholar who fell into a well while looking at the sky. Who does not, like them, laugh at this oxymoron: an absent-minded scholar, an inattentive expert, another Cosinus with glasses, a deaf Tournesol? By always looking up in the air, they never see where they put their feet. Body-less minds, everything is in their head and nothing below. Intellectuals in other words.

I too laughed for a long time, until one blessed day, a well-digging friend invited me to accompany him into the abyss. Our task was to control the quality of his scaffolding for building a masonry retaining wall, in a spot where the water was muddied by rubble. I no longer remember whether we used cable and winch as an elevator or if we went down rungs of crossbars inserted in the cylindrical side of the well. His professional and cheerful voice calmed my anxiety as it was getting dark, and we had to turn on our helmet lamps. As we arrived at the frame, a good twenty meters below ground, we discussed tech- niques and sturdiness. From time to time to boost my morale, I looked up to the small round light that heralded my impending renaissance, a second birth. And suddenly, I saw. Yes, the starry sky fell on my head. I recognized Vega and Lyre, no mistake. I was not dreaming. However, it was noon or almost noon during summer.

Wells 1

One day an astrologer
Fell down to the bottom of a well. He was told
Poor fool
When you can barely see your feet
You think you can read above your head?

Jean de la Fontaine "The Astrologer who fell down a well," *Fables, II, XIII*

"What am I seeing there above?" I asked my friend. "The stars of course!" "How is that possible", I stuttered. He laughed at my naivety. "See here, Michel", and he suddenly started giving me a lecture, "the long straight pipe in which we are plunged obliterates the global light of the now obscured sun. What remains visible are the constellations. The night's well reconstitutes the world's shadow."

I am not kidding, I was flabbergasted! In other words, the astronomer of the fable had not fallen into the well but had entered for professional reasons, to observe the stars and planets during the day. A true genius, he had invented, at least a thousand years before Galileo, a quasi-natural telescope hollowed out by one of his friends who was a mason. Those idiotic washerwomen, lying Greeks, stupid Æsop, that blabbermouth La Fontaine; those historians and men of letters without science, intellectuals without well-diggers: a plague on all of those who foolishly repeat an idiotic legend. "Yes," he said proudly, now becoming the artful specialist, "in areas with groundwater, we move in orbits whose clairvoyant eyes allow the earth to contemplate the mystical black body of the Universe."

I search in vain for a photographer who would follow a well-digger's descent into the center of the earth. From those underground telescopes he could give me a daylight look at the starry vault and not the superficial eye of an intaglio engraving of an ordinary blue sky.

View through a hole in the earth.

Wells II

A monster with Gorgon's eyes lies at the bottom of the well; no, not the nude woman Truth, nor the astronomer with the long view, but horror and desolation. A diabolical stench and confused screams emanate from the hole, together with reddish and yellowish flashes of lightning, demonic glimmers of the night. Whoever bends down over the edge, dies, struck down by the vertical and panoptical look of the dragon writhing in the inmost depths of Hell.

One day however, some hero, as lucid and handsome as St. Michael, rather smartly placed a mirror under the winch instead of a bucket and turned it towards the abyss. What do you think happened? Under its own evil spell, the hideous thing perished. Could Satan disappear by looking at himself with his evil eye?

Since then, we call it the well of Mirail, which, translated for Parisians, means mirror in the *langue d'oc.*

Opening inordinately wide, two intimidated eyes that are ready to cry and a mouth full of inoffensive teeth, this face inspires more pity than terror and makes you want to go to his rescue rather than submit to his ferocious will. This is a correct and healthy attitude to the divine that is destitute, feeble and frightened by human arrogance and anger.

Head of an Oceanian god, British Museum, London.

Narcissus-Torpedo

Do not immediately say Narcissus's well. His pretty name is derived from a dreadful poison, the torpid which can kill anyone with its electric discharge. As the Ancients knew about magnetism but not about electricity, their word *narke* in Greek, *torpedo* in Latin, evokes narcotics and torpor. Our ancestors thought the poison contained and projected a drug that induced sleep.

But do not think that the human Narcissus sleeps and dreams or even dies while looking at himself in the source with that well-known satisfaction. It might be possible, but not sufficient. He torpedoes, not himself, but his surroundings. Watch out for people in love with themselves: they quickly become dangerous for others whom they drug, fascinate, put to sleep, bombard with torpedoes and kill. Close to them, you are in mortal peril. Don't tell Narcissus this story, but if you have the misfortune of meeting one, try to turn the mirror upside down. Don't worry: they love themselves too much to die from looking at their reflection.

Do not trust the sweetness of an ecstatic Narcissus looking at his reflection in the water of a spring. In fact, narcissism is narcotic and first puts others to sleep before torpedoing them. Ναρκη, *narkè*, in Greek, is the name of a torpedo ray. Here Narcissus leaning forward is fascinated by the immobile image of the one he drowned.

Caravaggio, *Narcissus*, c. 1597-1599, Galleria nazionale d'Arte antica, Pallazzio Barberini, Rome.

Visit

Those wells and that source are immobile; Narcissus and the astronomer do not move. It is one thing to see but another thing to visit. As they run, basketball players see the hoop better than the spectators. Perhaps a driver going sixty miles an hour sees the landscape more distinctly than a painter holding his brush standing in front of his easel. When Alain Berthoz brilliantly discovered kinæsthesia, or moving vision, I danced with joy for having given the part on vision in my book *The Five Senses* the title "A visit: the itinerary of vision".

And so without landing once I visited Australia during a plane trip from New Zealand to Singapore. I never read a better drawn map of the globe, or a desert with better colors; I never saw a painting that was more perceptive, more completely and undisputedly abstract and concrete than those archaic dried-up former rivers, green and purple wash drawings, orange and yellowish streams, or dark punctuations in the middle of pigmented spots as shiny as lynx's eyes.

I never had a better view of our planet's face as it was millions of years ago. Below us, with a smile, the ancestral face of the Earth observed my eyes' juvenile travels. As parents we recognized each other.

In the nearby cabin, passengers with heavy eyelids and glasses, were yawning and watching a spaghetti western. Were they also sleeping with specs on their noses in Verne's old cavern?

Dusk near Uluru (Ayers Rock), solitude in the desert.
After sundown, a photographer emerges in a bush near me,
followed by a second one, and finally by a thousand of them
clicking at the bright red rock. The tourist brochure recommends
shooting the image at that moment of the day. Don't visit
sacred sites any longer: a tsunami of fellow men imitating
each other is flooding them.

Ayers Rock (or Uluru), Northern Territory, Australia.

Eye glasses

Clear-eyed about the human condition and about his journey to God or into nature, Spinoza had also formulated optical laws and explored the eye's physiology, like his master and model Descartes. Spinoza, I think, probably owed his perspicacity to the profession that made him living: he polished lenses for spectacles, a very sophisticated specialization in his time.

How could a significant part of humanity survive without this fantastic invention which makes you want to laugh at those grumpy people who say that instruments enslave you? Of course, a minuscule part of humanity would perhaps feel released from reading the books that I would be unable to write without this accessory. And also, knowing ophthalmologists tell us that a skilful and delicate surgical intervention under the eye will remove the Spinoza-inspired necessity to wear lenses in front of our eye-sockets. Right now, I bless those spectacles whose windows make far sighted people look younger.

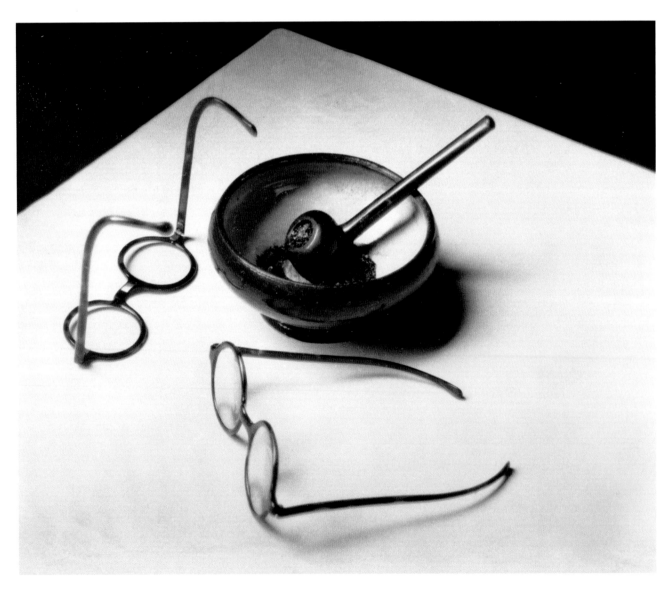

Surgical intervention as a work of art

A prince revered by ophthalmologists, Yves Pouliquen, member of the Académie Française, full of subtle humor, tells us that Monet, the revered prince of the Impressionists, did not have perfect vision, 1/10 in one eye and 2/10 in the other. Professor Coutelet, the master of Yves' master, decided to operate on the artist's cataracts. In those times – archaic in our eyes –, the surgeon bandaged the eye for eight days. It was out of the question to worry about what was going on underneath! A week later, Coutelat took off the bandage and asked Monet: "Do you see any better?" He answered: "My God, you are so ugly!"
In similar circumstances, Gulliver no longer had any desire to suckle after he discovered, as if under a microscope, the enormous breast of a giantess covered with boils and a mess of huge holes. In analogous circumstances, inversely, I heard René Girard exclaim with a dazzled smile: "Look, Michel, 'they' have repainted the world!"

This is not a pipe, but visibly a couple of glasses, spectacles that allows one to read.

André Kertész, *Mondrian's Glasses and Pipe*, photo from the series "France", 1926, Architecture and Heritage multimedia library, Charenton-le-Pont.

Let us look at beautiful or ugly, and now, small. Leibniz was mocking another great man: "I prefer, he said, someone like Leeuwenhoek who tells me what he sees, rather than a Descartes who tells me what he thinks." However full of clear ideas and distinct obvious facts as he said he was, the latter could not describe what the inventor of the microscope succeeded in showing for the first time: live beings he called *animalcules*, the first mono-cells, spermatozoids and ovules, whose combination made it possible to solve the old riddle of reproduction. Who could stand to see a landscape of millions of bacteria and viruses that cover, penetrate and individualize our bodies?

Let us think big. In the same period, maharajahs in India were building gigantic sun dials around Delhi to observe the sky. Those constructions were never used to tell time but were authentic astronomical observatories. Thanks to them, the ancient Greeks could invent the notion of latitude and even measure the earth's circumference fairly accurately. Hindu princes correctly thought to improve such measurements by increasing the size of those constructions. Alas, at the same time but thousands of miles away in Florence, Galileo had just invented the first telescope, whose accomplishments discredited those sun dials forever. Today tourists can go and see their magnificence and obsolescence and admire the monkeys that gambol among the creepers in the middle of the gradations.

Obliged to go along the banks of the Seine every day, I saw the four towers of the *Grande Bibliothèque* go up, projecting their shadow on me and I wondered if those builders had heard of the new technologies.

While history exonerates those ancient maharajas who were far removed from European innovations, what can we say about our contemporary princes who like all of us are familiar with the whole world. Just as we have telescopes orbiting around the earth to look at billions of galaxies, and each astronomer's computer functions as a singular observatory, data today, like books in the past, are less and less concentrated in rare and dense sites but more and more distributed to individual computers.

The multiplication, precision, sophistication and speed of our instruments now plunge us in an ocean, or rather tsunami, of scholarly, personal or informational data in numbers on such a scale that we do not yet know how to master, treat or theorize them. To conclude my argument, let me go back to Leibniz. Looking at the shelves of the "libraries" born with the invention of the printing press, he was wondering whether horrible masses of books would bring back barbarism or cultural renewal. Indeed, no one among us has ever seen or read all the books. And so, I am freed from libraries.

At that time, science made itself at home like a invited guest. From his simple chair, the astronomer observes the sky through an ordinary machine on a pedestal table in the living room. The visitor continues the conversation, as usual.

Sarvasiddhantatattvacudamani, The Jewel of the Essence of All Sciences, 1840, British Library, London.

Looking at the beautiful or the ugly, thinking big, thinking small

93

beech
eyes

Forest Beacons

Let us return to the dangerous narcissus, now a yellow or white flower. Let us look at this rusty beech tree which becomes a kaleidoscope with countless tints. No one looks at it and its beauty brings no one to a stop. It only displays this beauty in a secret explosion of calm splendor at this time of day, in the soft and humid autumn sunshine when night falls. Tomorrow, gusts of wind and rain will give it the right to lament. But at this moment, lost and hidden among its peers, it is radiant.

Each leaf mixes scarlet and olive tints and so it shines with a thousand eyes, irises and pupils, like a peacock whose every ocellus sees and is seen. Can a tree be a source releasing such a diverse and reserved inner glow that shines clearly and intensely? It discreetly lights up the dark green forest glade.

It is a scintillating look in the forest scattering; its beauty reveals the mute and modest clear-sightedness of an invisible God whom I would want to implore like this, upright, with closed eyes and my arms raised up to Him.

One has to dig deep into the animal kingdom to find sightless animals like bats and various types of moles. Whatever moves needs to find its bearings. Do plants look? Should I call them blind or seeing? I can see that trees have more eyes than we do. You must be joking. No! All living things owe their existence to the sun. In animals, their eyes link them to the light that trees receive through their leaves. Eyes and leaves have a similar destiny.

The November dusk is falling on the woods. Do I risk being taken by surprise by the shadow of the night? No, I am guided as on the sea by a thousand beacons scattered everywhere. Beech, sycamore and maple trees discreetly shed their lavish yellow, orange and scarlet red light on the paths, adding a bit more daylight. During the summer, sun rays nourish the leaves; programmed to fall to the ground in autumn, they still keep traces of the colors of the star now fragmented in little pieces on the ground. The glimmers now come from below; less from the leaves that still hang loosely on branches like tattered rags than from the dead leaves with their brilliant colors. The summer nights are dark while the fall evenings shine brightly.

Like forest beacons, trees now multiplied on the ground, sweepingly guide my eyes with their reddish wedges that sparkle feebly. In the summer, green trees close their eyelids; in the fall, they lament the loss of their leaves and dot the earth with red eyes, which grants them multiple vision.

Dead and lively, this stump thrusts its roots down so deeply that in French it became the name for the common ancestors of a species, bacteria and viruses, the cells of each organism, our families, tribes and nations, languages and dialects, buildings supports or stone foundations ... and even for stubs of notebook pages. The universal mother.

The panoptic in the spring

In Costa Rica, that narrow strip in Central America, on top of a *cerro* or a volcano in the Talamanca range perched almost 4000 meters high, you can see in one glance the Gulf of Mexico to the east and the Pacific Ocean to the west. Similarly, in Northern California, on top of the Borel Hill, you can see the ocean on one side and the San Francisco Bay on the other side. There are obviously central spots in the world that have better eyes than anywhere else.

In the middle of spring, the meadows around such spots, like the hills of the lower Alps, are dotted with garlands of flowers with so many colors that my eyes cannot count them. I swear that the longest dictionary of color catalogues could not mention them all. With its particular cosmetic concocted in the secret alchemy of its genes, each floral tint attracts the eyes and wings of bees and bumblebees, those pollinating messengers. Each flower opens up expectantly and with each color shamelessly displays its desire to be fertilized.

Divided by time and expectation, united by hope and desire, I recognize in these dotted meadows my own scented and colored soul. The hope emanating from the soil's surface lifts it up; it flies away like the mottled wing of a butterfly. I fly on that wing. Or inversely, the rainbow descends on it. Its dappled display broadens my soul as it flies.

If you have never seen an Indian summer in the forests of Quebec north of Montreal and around Chesapeake Bay in Maryland, you have not yet experienced the ecstatic plenitude of a gaze. Inversely, how many thousands of marvels have these thousands of maple trees seen in the sky to explode into thousands of purple, scarlet and crimson shades?

Mont Orford, Quebec.

Spring awakening

The previous day a
thousand white stars were
shining on the mountain
slope: daisies, red and blue
gentians, flaming pink and
purple foxgloves, as well
as *Arnica Montana.*
All disappeared when the
dull grey dusk descended.
In the dark, flowers sleep.
Somnus plantarum, wrote
Linnaeus, who centuries
later copied Albert
the Great who himself was
condemned, poor soul,
for having committed the
sin of animism with this
expression.
Suddenly, the south-facing
slope wakes up and the
mountain pasture is dotted
with shiny dappled colors.
The mountain opens its eyes
which are now as heavily
spangled as those of a fly.

Carried away by words? In any case, beech wood burns quickly and its flame leaves few ashes; nothing is more practical for a baker's oven. In the past beech was called "bakery wood."

Gustav Klimt, *Beech Forest*, 1908, Museum of Art, Linz.

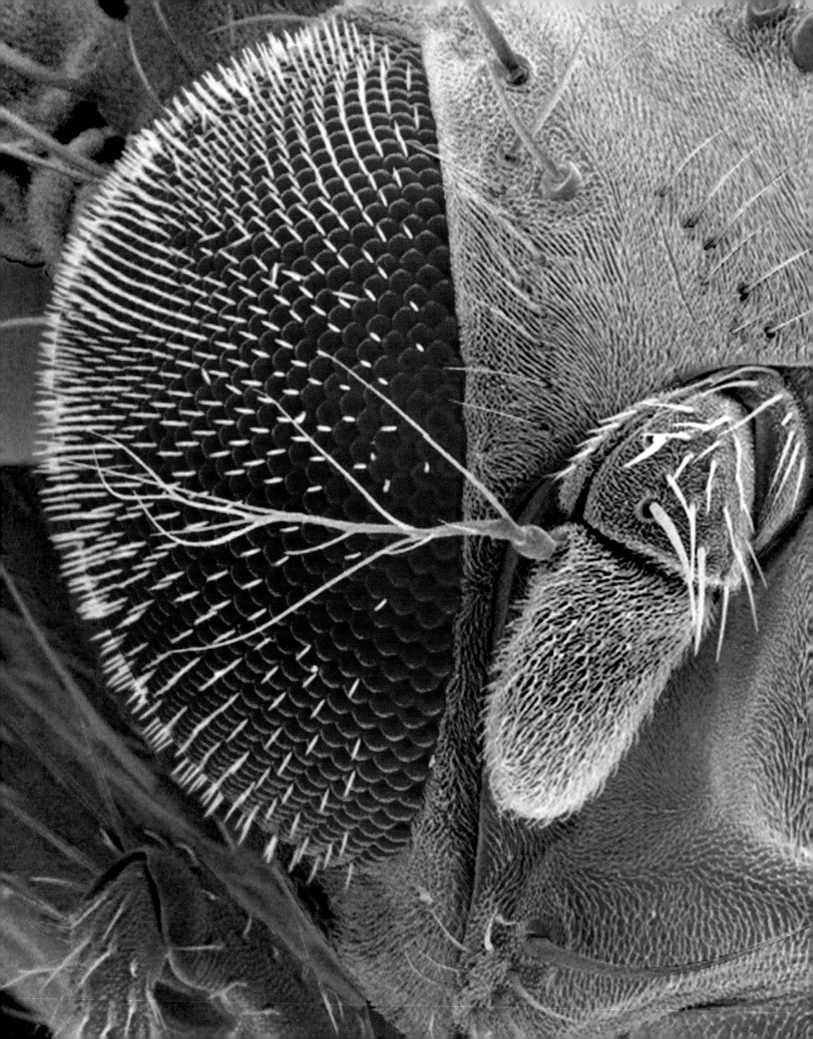

animal
eyes

Diving

Immobile between two waters, the sea perch is the only creature capable of the ecstasy of stopping without stirring up its surroundings. It looks around with calm, deep and almost melancholic eyes. What do those huge pupils contemplate with their unbearable brilliance and superhuman serenity?

It seems to examine itself with sadness, to reflect with resignation on its monotonous life. It is a bitter world where one has either to eat with wide-open gills or be eaten by an even wider opening, kill or be killed, pathetically subjected to this unspeakable original sin. What does this barely open mouth seem to complain about or deplore? It has so much to say but cannot, deprived as it is of language.

It looks about to cry but the oppressive seawater seems to stop it. Its species has shed so many tears that it swims in a sea of tears. Schools of other fish move close by with grieving mouths, sad eyes, drowning in their own sobs. Have I ever understood the sea's bitterness?

I remember those dusks on the deck, when holding a sextant I waited for a star to light up to take our bearings. I would sometimes shift my glance to the sea itself, whose unique eye like a green spherical abyss ecstatically contemplates God's blue darkness with bitter tears.

The melancholy expressed by fish eyes, whose sadness is linked to their muteness, moves me so much that I am unable to say what I have to say, even though I have said a lot. Their clenched jaws, that language muzzle, makes me and them cry so much that our tears fill the sea.

Common sea perch, Spain.

The beach

I was recently walking at daybreak, alone surrounded by vultures and sea lions, along a California shore. I was going back and forth when I noticed a seal following along as I walked; it kept looking at me, replicating in the ocean my pedestrian semi-circular route around the bay. I thought I was observing it, but was it observing me? Who was watching whom, as both of us were traveling along the transparent orbit of the beach?

This is how I go about in the world whose stars, stones, leaves or feral cats never cease looking at me.

The majestic chicken with the little duck

Chicken still lay eggs, but supposedly they are no longer able to sit on them since the industrial mass production of eggs began. In the past we used to put them delicately in oval wicker baskets lined with comfortable straw padding, where we gently laid down two dozen eggs. I do not know if the chicken were sleeping, but hot from their hard-working body, they no longer preened their feathers and it looked like they were growing old. We fed them moist grain and even gave them some hooch at times to warm them up. When the yellowish-white chicks, practically blind, punctured the shells with their beaks and appeared forty days later, the new mother clucked happily, less proudly but more calmly than when they laid their eggs. The new-borns scattered unsteadily around the farmyard while the hen ran sleepily around limping, trying to gather them under her.

Less gentle and less maternal, there were fewer ducks on the farm to do this job. So we slipped their eggs under the hens' bottoms. When all the eggs were hatched, the various chicks were part of the same brood. The den mother and the cubs had no clue except when at some point in time – I no longer know exactly when – the ducklings rushed genetically towards the duck pond. God himself could not stop their aquatic instinct.

You should see the mother's panic when dizzy, anxious and trembling, she sees her offspring, normally creatures of the land, plunge into such a foreign element. She screams pitifully, loses her balance and shakes her bristling feathers. I will forever remember that poor animal's haggard, terrified and flashing eyes and its superhuman look of affection and panic. The hen looked like a *Pietà* with chicken eyes.

I was born into a family that had no books and whose culture was limited to evening prayer. I still hear my distressed mother exclaiming as she saw me read: "I am a hen who hatched a duck." Did she have that same look?

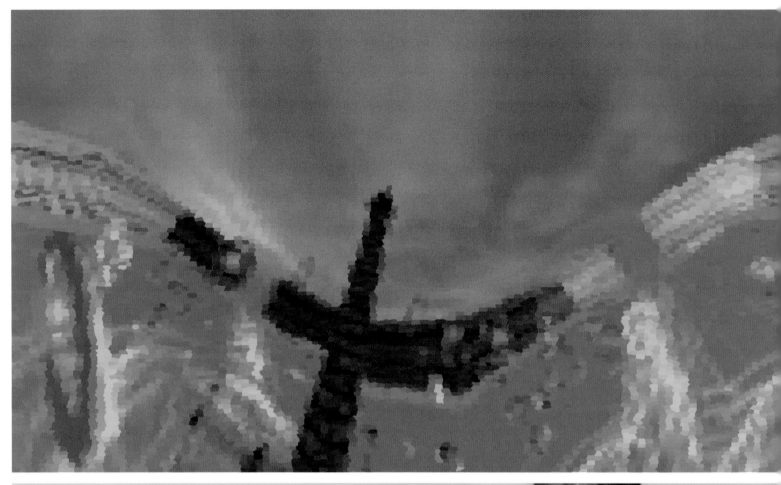

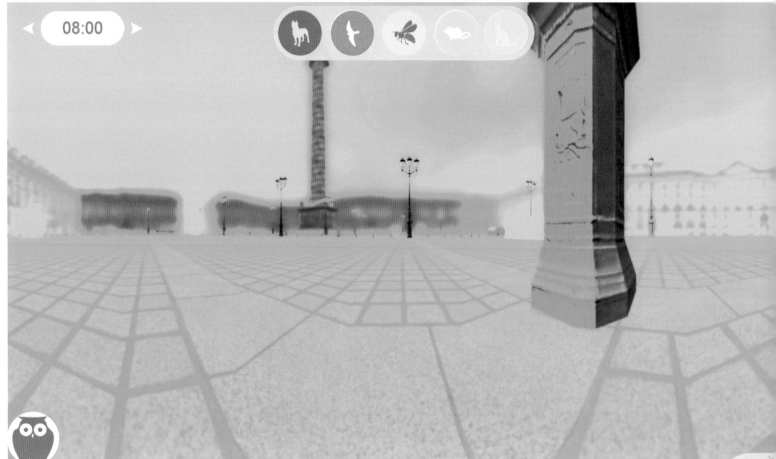

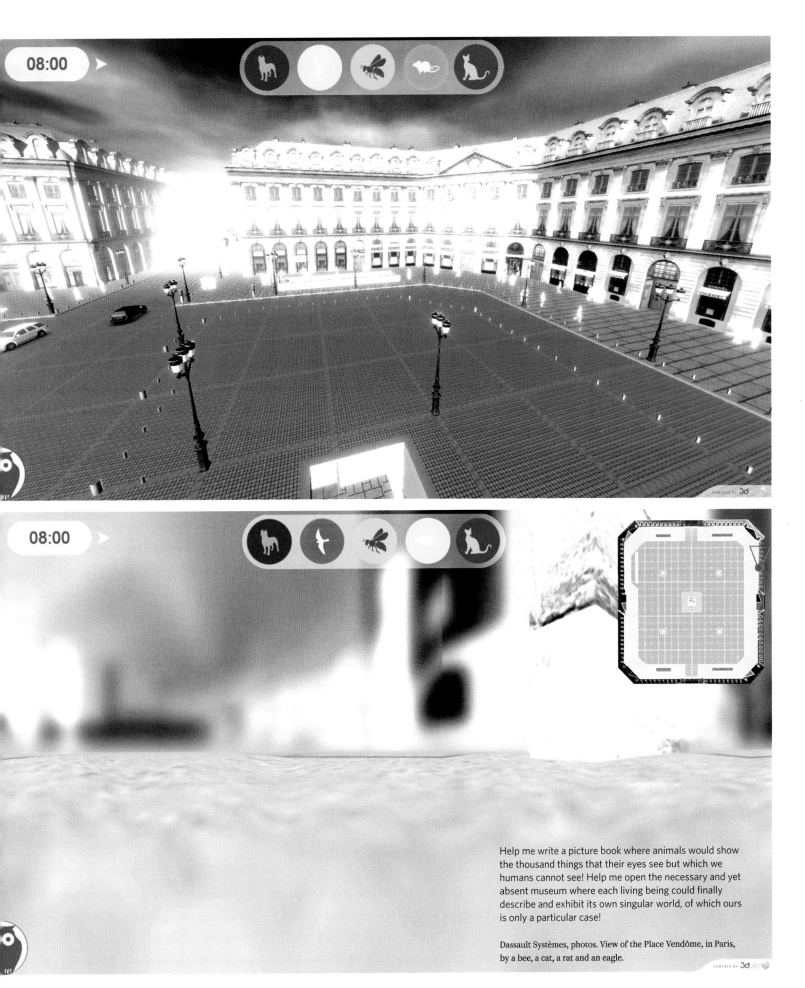

Help me write a picture book where animals would show the thousand things that their eyes see but which we humans cannot see! Help me open the necessary and yet absent museum where each living being could finally describe and exhibit its own singular world, of which ours is only a particular case!

Dassault Systèmes, photos. View of the Place Vendôme, in Paris, by a bee, a cat, a rat and an eagle.

I recall one afternoon at the Sydney Zoo where, leaning against the wire fence gorilla cage, I felt a huge male of my age, with white hair, leaning against my back. He chewed some leaves while I sucked on candies. Like fellow classmates, we were staring at each other and imitating our mimics and grimaces; we stayed together for hours like happily laughing friends. Who was seeing himself in a mirror?

Young pigmy chimpanzee in front of a swing mirror.

Animals

Karl von Frisch once told me that bees see beyond the spectrum of colors perceived by humans, below and above the rainbow. I would also like to know how the world is drawn and colored for flies; it is probably multiplied by its compound eyes. What universe do those big bull's eyes reveal? They must see far enough away for our architects to have called bull's eyes attic imposts. On the other hand fighting bulls are nearsighted; they do not see very far and run to their death because of their poor sight and human cruelty. How can we be just and sympathetic in our treatment of animals if we do not try to see the world they discover and which their lives build for them? Why do we take pity on the lamb, bled to death at the slaughterhouse? Why however do we light-heartedly crush mosquitoes and woodlouse? And yet they all have eyes! Do they have tears too?

Here is the imaginary museum of the *Biogea,* the dream of an exhibit this book would open. As there are millions of species on Earth, they must live in as many different worlds, feel millions of perceptions, and see millions of drawings, colors, canvasses and paintings that are different from ours. *Biogea's* museum would reproduce icons perceived by city rats and drawn by field rats, and also the colored images produced by the immense zoo of sighted animals: seagulls, stags, rattlesnakes, and spiders. Oh, imagine seeing the *Fables de la Fontaine* illustrated by the animals themselves, in the Louvre for wolves, or *Oaks* and *Reeds* in the art gallery for *Pine* trees. Oh! To see my book illustrated by the chaotic infinity of those strange views.

First, the word *culture* has two meanings; the official one, which tells us to visit the Louvre, and the ethnological, which describes tribes and customs. However, just as Cervantes associates Don Quixote drunk on books with a potbellied Sancho on his mule, so Hubert Robert often paints shepherdesses milking their goats in a dismantled museum. This is the only valid meaning of the word, where real culture puts a stable in the Sorbonne.

Hubert Robert, *Le Retour du troupeau*, v. 1773-1775, The Metropolitan Museum of Art, New York.

You do not enter or leave because you are always already there. There are just labels that indicate the type of rock you carelessly trample on, or the kind of thorn that almost injured you, and the kind of habitat occupied by such and such a living species that is absent for the moment and considered dangerous. You look, you experience and cross the surrounding desert. You could visit it here and now because its inhabitants and habitats have been framed, classified, designated and named according to the method of Linnaeus. You could have heard stones speak and heard serpents and spiders converse. Here is my fabulous *Biogea* museum finally realised, outside, right in the middle of the Australian outback! I saw myself turning into a real Aboriginal, dancing and tattooed.

Oh shades of Hubert Robert, you wanted to destroy the walls of the Grand Gallery in the Louvre to insert shepherdesses and oxen in the hollow of the ruins; you wanted to enlarge the windows until the walls had disappeared. You accompanied me on my dream visit into this *Biogean* enchantment that opened so wide as to ignore the walls framing the holes that would have blocked our view.

Finally we really see Life and the Universe.

Panoptic

How did the peacock's feathers get studded with ocelli?

Once upon a time, there was a man everyone called Argus, who was

said to have two pairs of eyes: one on his face, like everyone else and the

other in the back of his head. Of course he did not know what a blind spot was.

The same myth also whispered that while he openly showed his four pupils and eyelids,

in fact there were another hundred hidden eyes scattered about the surface of his skin.

And so Argus could see everywhere, from every angle and position but more than that, he was always looking since he only slept half dozing, half-awake with half-closed eyelids. This all-seeing guard deserved his real but more secret name *Panoptes*, the panoptic: he who sees everything.

In those divine and mythical days, Zeus, the king of Gods, has just fallen in love with Io. Jealous of her womanizing husband, his wife, Queen Hera keeps a relentless watch over him. The most powerful of all the gods, the lover eludes his wife's all-seeing surveillance by transforming things and people. He changes Io into a heifer and himself into a bull. And so we have quadruped lovemaking – from behind.

Zeus makes his move and Hera is checkmated.

Knowing his divine power to take on a thousand possible shapes as he wishes, the queen is suspicious of the horned animal whose muzzle is snuffling around the smooth coat of the beautiful heifer. Hera herself enjoys a similar power; she becomes a horsefly that pursues the heifer incessantly with its sting. Maddened by the pain of the repeated stabbing, Io gallops away, pursued by the insect, crosses Europe through valleys and mountains, swims across a sea, which of course becomes the Ionian sea. To escape the pain, she jumps over a strait, now the Bosphorus, i.e., the cow's passage, and finally ends up bemoaning her destiny of having been loved by the god, with Prometheus. He had been chained to a rock in the Caucasus and devoured by a vulture because he too was hated by those who madden the ones they wish to destroy and especially their favored or loved ones.

Hera plays Io and drives her crazy; now Zeus is checkmated.

However, the queen loses sight of species and elements. She knows that

Jupiter once changed into a swan to love Leda and even into a

golden rain to penetrate Danae's vagina in tumbling waves.

Worried, anxious and nervous, she scrutinizes every-

thing that moves.

This is an allegory for our times. On the left, Panoptes, the guard with the thousand eyes embedded in his body; on the right, Hermes flooding space with Muzak. Who wins? Hearing of course, which has triumphed in pedagogy and cognition, but also in banal commercial practices. So noted. Just a moment however, who is showing this triumph? The answer is: an obviously mute painting.

Pinturicchio, Io, *Argus and Mercury*, beginning of the 16th century, Borgia apartments.

Everything can be a god;
yes everything is a god: that is the
metamorphic secret of pantheism.
Would Zeus hide in the shape
of a horsefly?
Mistrusting everything leads
to madness. This has happened
to many philosophers.
Now Hera has gone mad and is
in turn checkmated.
To get help, she summons
Panoptes, the all-seeing detective,
an excellent warden and merciless
disciplinarian. Like the Grand
Inquisitor, nothing escapes his
prying. His gaze which defies time
and space, can see through
successive metamorphoses.
He is able to recognize a god in
an animal, a goddess in a river,
one thing in another because,
constantly vigilant, he has seen
the changes. Piercing the invisible,
the divine panoptic guesses
and betrays divine strategies.
Hera plays Panoptes; now Zeus
is checkmated.
Now Zeus summons Hermes.
Hera's jealousy obtains help
from policing which establishes
the omnipresence of looks,
globalizes the encyclopaedic totality
of all possible representations
on all imaginable screens.
The newcomer integrates all
communications, commerce,
messages, thieves, treacherous liars
and faithful translators, roads and
crossroads, networks and all sorts
of data. It is a struggle of giants:
pixels against beeps, one totality
against another.
In the war between the god and the
goddess, the final battle has started.
Hermes invents his weapon:
Pan's flute. Pan against Panoptes.
Competition between the senses:
sight against hearing; the fight
between the media: the image
versus sound.
Hermes advances openly and faces

Panoptes. He sits next to him and far from attacking him, he plays his flute. The viewer listens. Who hears when we listen to music? the body, yes; all the senses, yes; the mind, yes again. No other practice can engage the whole self like this. Music unites. Everything in us hears; nothing in us is left behind by sound waves. We are completely gripped, subjugated, fascinated and ecstatic, either fully awake or asleep, it does not matter. The panoptical globe is overturned and the sphere of sight is undermined. Panoptes shakes his head, dozes off and begins to cry;

his eyes cloud over with sleep and tears; his sight blinded by sobs, his clairvoyance is disrupted. He can no longer see. Hermes gets up and kills him. Hera is checkmated and Zeus remains king. I revere Hermes, the hero of our era, but I hate his battle. Doesn't he ever shed tears? This appalling myth of jealousy and killing is drenched in tears and lamentations. As in life and death, love is lost in competition and cries of suffering. Argus cries, Hera cries and Io cries... floods of tears flow from all eyes, even those of the panoptic.

The gods' lofty residence, Mount Olympus, which used to be invulnerable, is foundering now that love's disenchantment has set in. All the world's eyes are crying. Mourning and humiliated, Hera is said to have found a bird, rendered featherless by disappointed love. She stripped Panoptes of his skin strewn with eyelids and pupils and gave it to the peacock whose feathers since then have been dotted with ocelli. It cannot fly but instead fans out its tail. It looks at us bitterly with its dead spangled eyes weeping over our lost loves.

Mythology describes how Panoptes, covered with eyes, was changed into a male peacock whose extended tail is studded with ocelli. This reciprocal equivalence shows that the Ancients knew that we do not just see with our eyes. If not, why say ocelli?

*literary
eyes*

Eyes with nodes

At the top of the political pyramid or the Eiffel Tower, the emperor, president, the Sun King, Juno or Jupiter – in other words, the master's eye – stands guard and watches. As a counterpart to the monotheistic rule of an unimaginable God whose image is forbidden, its Pupil shines in the middle of a triangle. Surveillance, supervision, this omnipresent God looks at Cain even in his tomb.

Today, we leave behind this very strident outline of the old world. However, worried that we cannot clearly see the new one, we wonder how society will be organized when multiple networks produce a multitude of roads and crossroads, each functioning more or less as an apex. There is an eye in each of these intersections or nodes. Each network shines with a countless number of different gazes that are more or less awake. All these countless orbits, each of them, permanently look at each other all the time. In other words, the totality looks at the totality; countless numbers permanently watch over countless numbers. No, we are no longer the focus of scrutiny and have somehow become under-scrutinized. We do not know yet what those gazes mean, nor what they see or how they are organized. We only know that they exchange gigantic volumes of information that is indeed transparent, hidden however by an immense chaos.

Why does an impeccable and rational order end up criminal? How does the most refined culture vanish into barbarism? Why does organization end up in chaos? We old Europeans can no longer see these images again without nausea.

Benito Mussolini presiding over a gymnastics competition in a Rome stadium, 1934.

The older, less populated and more concentrated world was organized according to the old Latin saying *Omnes in unum*: all federated in one, recruited by the apex, all focussed on one chief, one head, one goal or objective, a top of a pyramid, or in short, on the unique God, the eye in the center of the triangle. Nothing was easier than this focal solution that we sometimes called value or reference. There was nothing more stable over time than this pyramidal form, whose apex was given the name of either the chief or the ideal. Unfortunately this was our own experience and history shows us that it was paid for with martyrdom, sacrifice, lynching, everyone's heroism, people ready and summoned to give their lives to fight to the death for this unity. What price the glory that history worships in these killers: Achilles, Alexander, so-called the Great, Julius Caesar, Louis, also called the Great, Napoleon, Stalin, Mao? The density of rays surrounding them probably produces such heat that all the bodies carbonize as if in a furnace.

Let us turn our backs on these deaths for once and leave the past. Networks replace pyramids and the web the Eiffel Tower. We are trying to guess how democracy will replace the old focused and unitary framework.

Putting this photo together with the preceding one leads to a strange notion: do we have to read the first as the consequence of large numbers, as the result of the second? What can be done about such a multitude, besides containing it? How can the world's density be organized, when between those two images it went from two to eight billion souls humming through a hundred networks?

Passing along safety ramps, Beijing station, May 2014.

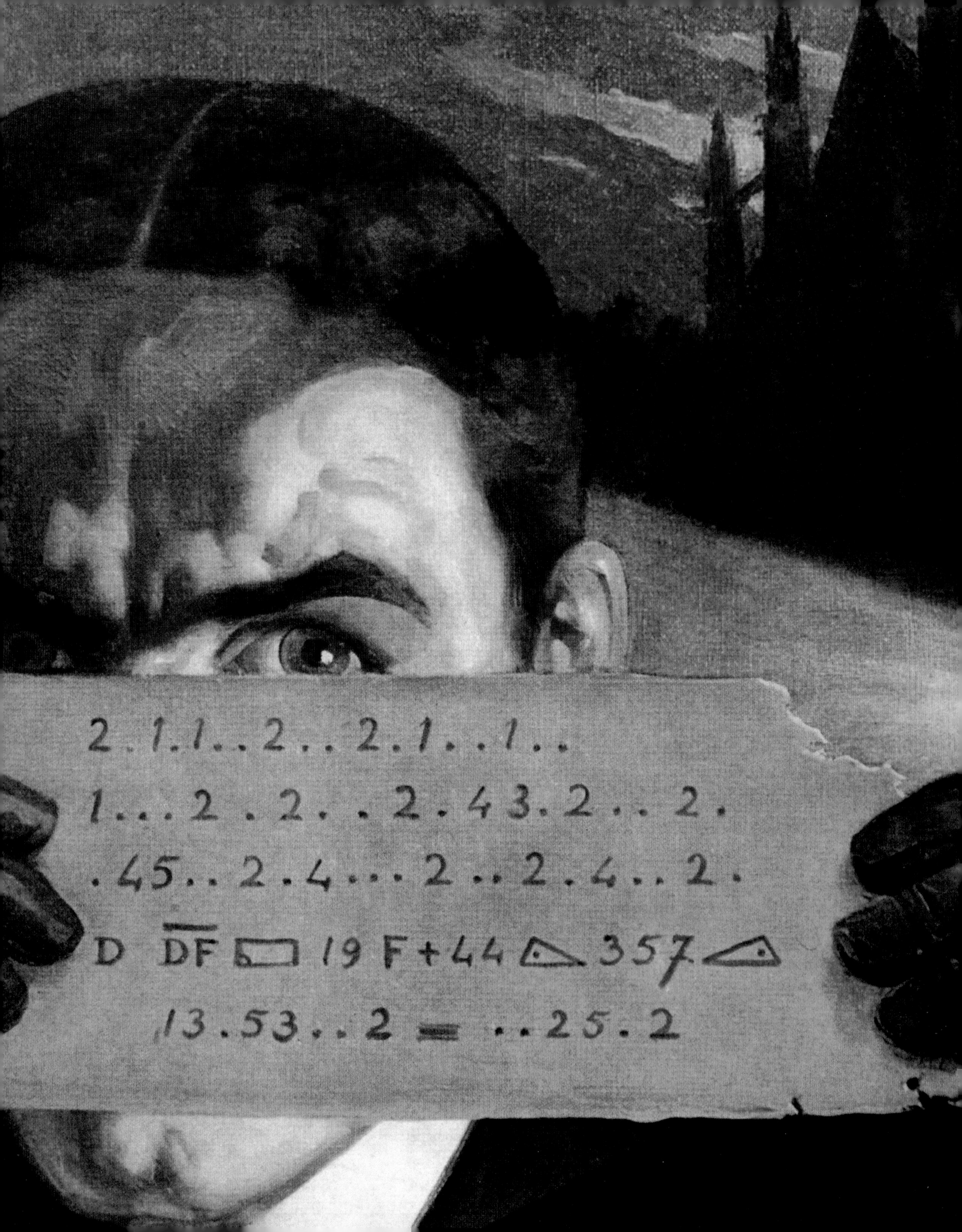

Eyes of dots and dashes

Only old sailors and scouts remember scot or morse. Like binary notation, formed with a 1 and a 0, the alphabet of these obsolete languages consisted of dots called *ti* and dashes called *ta*. *Ti-ta* becomes the *a*; *ti ti* becomes the *i*; *tata ta*, the o and so on. Transmitted by telegraph the sounds of morse were long or short while scot sent long or short flashes to the eyes. Sailors who were well trained in transmission understood this alphabet as quickly and clearly as their mother tongue. We midshipmen chatted in scot as fluently as a graduate student or a priest could then debate in Latin.

To evade all surveillance, we had invented a wink with one eye for a dot and with two eyes for a dash. Messages passed through everywhere, secretly and quickly without the guards suspecting anything. No need to hide; we just needed to look each other in the eye. At school those talented in mathematics could give their classmates the results of nautical calculations, while the rowdy elements could tell their jokes to provoke laughter without anyone understanding where the outburst came from. No need for a semaphore or a telephone to make appointments. These furtive signs flying around signalled a team's complicity, a community spirit and sometimes the joy of belonging.

As a young sailor on the merry sea, I guessed at the power, virtual might and lightning speed of multitudes in a communication network. Looking into each other's eyes, together we had experienced half a century before the web how democracy could be established in life, how the multiple could be unified or in Jean-Jacques Rousseau's words, how democracy could serve the general will. The master's eye could be forgotten and his watch defied.

Will we one day know how to generalise for large numbers the perpetual rapturous movement in which the virtuous circle of two eyes enlivens and enchants lovers?

Deciphering illegible scrawls is a good small-scale model for any story: Balzac, Poe, Verne, Hergé and many others have used it. Suspense and denouement are indeed similar to the long and difficult decoding of an encrypted text. When Turing was able to decipher the secret messages of the Nazi military, the war was virtually finished.

Maurice Leblanc, *The Hollow Needle*.

Playful eyes

Playing doctor, children receive their first lesson in comparative anatomy. What a discovery! Will the day come when such examinations cease? The name of this game is not accidental, because the view of sex, especially that of the other's sex, has curative effects: all our life, we feel its therapeutic need. What is curiosity? A good cure.

In a team sport, the unquestionable advantage of the home game is measured by the volume and power of ten or forty thousand eyes dispersed in a concentric stadium, directed towards the group of eleven or fifteen that strives to fight with hands or feet against an adversary deprived of those converging glances.

In past centuries, experts argued for a long time whether eyes received light or emitted it. Optics settled the issue in an instant. I cannot go back on a decision that has been confirmed over and over again by science and experience. But having played in teams of five or fifteen in front of a favourable or hostile public, I must confess how much we were carried along or slowed down by an almost noticeable heat, by an almost tangible force, a kind of horsepower.

Just as a flame can shoot up from light rays focussed on "burning mirrors," like those with which Archimedes supposedly set fire to the enemy fleet… similarly, the convergence of those eyes on our white or blue shirts inspired us with greater energy. This energy was so inspiring that we could only win against stronger adversaries who did not have this collective focus.

The so-called entertainment society does not describe an abstraction or a set of illusions but, on the contrary, a power that can be evaluated. Political power is born in the circus.

Could reality possibly be born from representation?

What kind of public, what encounter is this, for the spectators
to remain so uptight? No arms up in the air, there is no wild gesture,
no parody, no Mexican wave travestie...
I would be cruelly disappointed if I had to play in the team that
these policemen watch so apathetically.

Even a policeman is still a man or an expert in painting.

Robert Doisneau, *Romy's Shop Window*, 1948.

stage
eyes

With its thousand forms and colors, Harlequin's coat apparently refers to a cutting-up of the body, that was called *diasparagmos,* where the victim's body was torn apart into different limbs. Likewise, actors on stage feel like mincemeat, chopped up by the spectators' looks, but also reunified in their own community.

Paper for cut-outs, Popular Art, c. 1850, MuCEM, Marseilles.

The show is on. Harlequin's costume is so fascinating that it often appears before my eyes. Just as the fly presents two multifaceted eyes, so this comic figure wears the result of multiple looks. By parading so often before so many people, his costume is marked by traces left by a million gazes. He is even supposed to have reigned as the Emperor of the Moon, which means he traveled around plural worlds. As each gaze has seen a singular world, their variety is expressed in each of the multi-colored and multi-facetted patches of his coat. Losing his identity, Harlequin joins the multitude: "I am multiple", he says, "my soul with its hundreds of voices sings like a sonorous echo; my heart with thousands of colors sparkles like a broken mirror; my body with its hundreds of forms is meta-morphosed. Like a diamond it explodes in many tints while my eyes reflect the rays of innumerable viewers, whether they be lucid, one-eyed or curious. I am a stone among stones, an oak in an oak forest, an animal among animals, a person immersed in the people, plunged among all living beings and their analogue and I live in Verne's cavern". In parentheses: here I recite my *Cogito*.

Moreover, my own loose and flowing coat changes and is transformed. Its colors and forms become more varied and an increasing number of the coat's pieces shrink and become infinitely small. At the limit of the infinitely small, the fabric acquires a dazzling white color and so the lunar Pierrot appears. The color white adds, integrates and subsumes all colors. This is the candidate, so named since the dawn of our language because he is dressed in a garment of pristine white.

The Celebrity's face

Stoned to death by a thousand archers, pierced by arrows, Saint Sebastian represents one scapegoat among others. Change those spears into looks and you have celebrities who expose themselves to be admired but also risk public prosecution. The summit of glory, the Capital is close to the Tarpean rock from which victims were thrown to the bottom.

Andrea Mantegna, *The Martyrdom of Saint Sebastian*, detail, 1490, Galleria Giorgio Franchetti alla Ca' d'Oro, Venice.

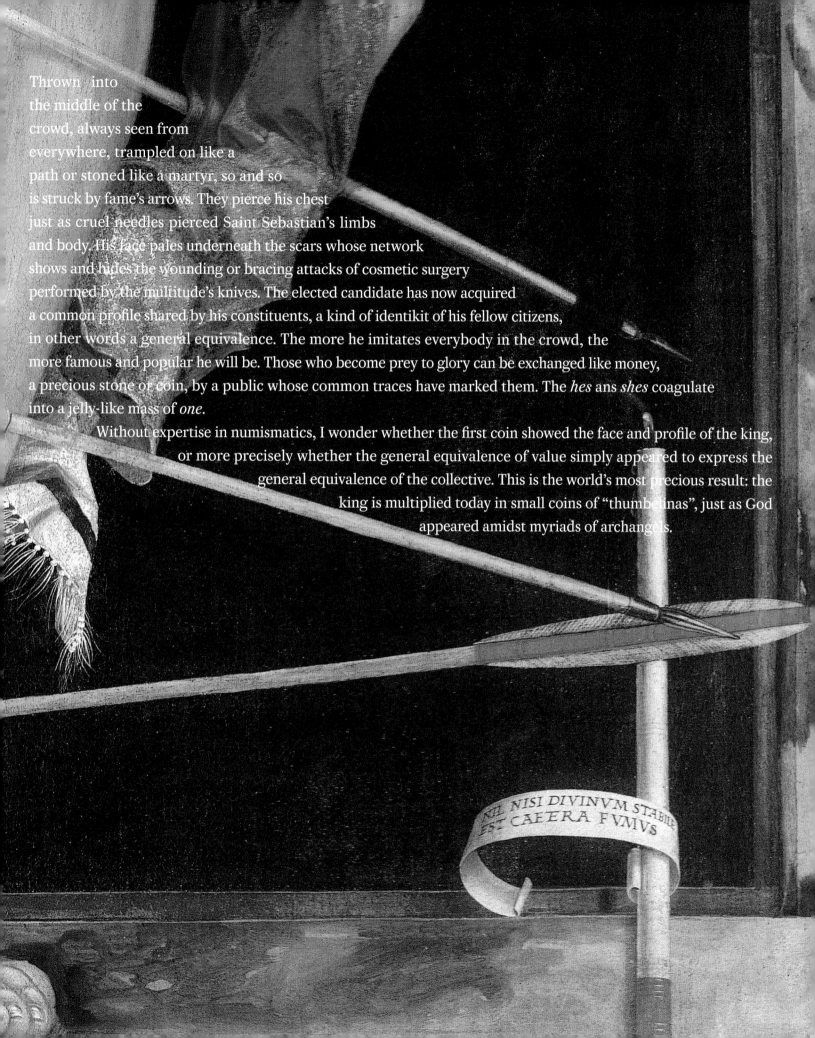

Thrown into
the middle of the
crowd, always seen from
everywhere, trampled on like a
path or stoned like a martyr, so and so
is struck by fame's arrows. They pierce his chest
just as cruel needles pierced Saint Sebastian's limbs
and body. His face pales underneath the scars whose network
shows and hides the wounding or bracing attacks of cosmetic surgery
performed by the multitude's knives. The elected candidate has now acquired
a common profile shared by his constituents, a kind of identikit of his fellow citizens,
in other words a general equivalence. The more he imitates everybody in the crowd, the
more famous and popular he will be. Those who become prey to glory can be exchanged like money,
a precious stone or coin, by a public whose common traces have marked them. The *hes* ans *shes* coagulate
into a jelly-like mass of *one*.

Without expertise in numismatics, I wonder whether the first coin showed the face and profile of the king,
or more precisely whether the general equivalence of value simply appeared to express the
general equivalence of the collective. This is the world's most precious result: the
king is multiplied today in small coins of "thumbelinas", just as God
appeared amidst myriads of archangels.

NIL NISI DIVINVM STABIL
EST CAEERA FVMVS

The face is seen and sees

Look at the face of a star seen by millions of viewers: a politician, a movie star, a television host, a talented player in a team sport, a popular *musac* singer, in short the face of a celebrity. Depersonalized, sometimes bruised like an overripe pear, the face shows a bloated skin like that of a drunk or a whore whose slightly puffy planes and livid pallor serve as an armour against the incessant attacks of the public. It is as if this impersonal barrier had become the transparent sum of innumerable looks it received or the blankness of its own vague stares directed to nobody in particular, except perhaps at the entire crowd, a collective unit endowed with a life of its own. The theatre mask of a comedy or tragedy which the Ancients called *persona* is modelled on the social dynamic forcing the erasure or effacement of a personality for the benefit of those who admire, acclaim or detest it. Does it reflect them? Each of us can wear such a mask or mirror.

Did Jean-Jacques Rousseau ever imagine that the general will, the transparent sum of all individual intentions, would ever have been so clearly inscribed on the legislator's face, or would be projected on the candidate's costume, in Rome the white toga?

In the past, a theatre mask had two functions: it served as a megaphone and to caricature a character that spectators could recognize from afar. Hence its name of *persona*.

Theatre mask, 1st century BC, Museo archeologico nazionale, Taranto.

The Halo

What the Greeks called *kudos*, and what today we
call charisma – still a Greek word – does not originate in a
charismatic person who would project it as a thousand suns, but
instead it is projected mirror-like on the crowd's reflection that
receives back what it has cast. The face and body of the candidate, the
elected official, the legislator or the celebrity, are imprinted with all the
power of the public in proportion to its huge numbers. The Sun King gives back
to his subjects the rays he has received from them. Rebounding from the body of
Saint Sebastian, the arrows go directly to the hearts of those who shot them. The
victim becomes conqueror or king; the Tarpeian rock becomes the Capitol. He who has
just been stoned now has a pile of rocks, a powerful reserve of efficient weapons. So many
thoughts are suggested by the respective etymologies of the word *sub-jectus*, the subject
lying under the stones thrown at him, and by the term *suffrage*, the operation that places the
elected officials under the same fragments! Do they too have projectiles?

Political power originates from these exchanges and the metamorphosis of many into one and
from one into many, but does it come from the people or on the contrary from the tyrant, the
aristocracy, the rich or from God? This no doubt a classic question in political science, remains
superficial because it merely classifies, whereas in reality power both in the sense of what is possible or virtual, but also in the sense of physical and dynamic force, is ceaselessly transformed from
group violence, and the vanity or courage of those who resist it, into the force of one or several
individuals. In proportion to its numbers and aggressiveness, this heat, violence and capacity to move,
always originates from multiplicity: from where else would its fluctuating volumes and quantity
originate? Whether political power is stolen or given back, it is always changed into violence and
oppression or mastery and freedom. The pallor of the face and the body becomes the mirror reflecting and returning the rays to those who emit them and receive them transformed. All power lies in
this exchange and in the transubstantiation between emitters and receivers.

The halo poses the same problem as the eye in the past: either light emanates from the saint's painted head or the painter projects it on the head. Either the character exudes charisma or genius gushes forth from the artist. As an alternative, I choose the circle: the genius of the painter consists in seeing that his flaming model sees him through the halo just as he sees him through the gaze.

Simone Martini, *Maestà*, 1315, Museo civico, Palazzo pubblico, Sienna.

In the realms of politics, the media, education, justice and medicine, the ancient world had few emitters and huge numbers of receivers. Hence the pyramidal scheme. The new networked world has as many emitters as receivers. The new collectives imitate the world of Verne's cavern where it would be impossible to distinguish one central gem or source among the network of exchanges of brilliant flashes of color and intense lights. In our collective or political night we are all emitting and receiving stars and planets. Through communication networks each of us has all possible power.

What will we do with it tomorrow?

Diffuse light, a dance, colorful robes, ecstatic faces, wings ready to fly, the field studded with flowers in rainbow colors, a circle of dancers holding hands in an eternally returning present: this is how Fra Angelico sees the serenity of Paradise.

Guido di Pietro aka Fra Angelico, *The Last Judgment*, painting on wood, detail, 15th century, convent of San Marco, Florence.

Eloquence, debates and spectacles

I am familiar with the dynamics of those reciprocal transformations or reflections that can become heated and explosive only in the form of the spoken word. In the course of my professional life I have discovered that eloquence consists in responding forcefully, but as harmoniously as possible, to the silent stares focussed on the speaker as if returning and reflecting their preciously attentive listening. The voice is only there to transform the listeners' silence, sometimes their exhaustion, sometimes their enthusiasm when the rhetoric is sublime. Sun and planet, the eloquent orator receives arrows and sends them back either changed to his advantage or to his detriment. He conceitedly awaits a standing ovation but fears a fiasco. Whether a tyrant's triumph or an emissary's humiliation, it is the same deception.

Let him change this method and allow the public to speak; have him scorn meaningful and violent eloquence in order to become the mediating pivot of the debate. The intersection of the speakers' interventions will then be his response. Questions often produce answers. In so doing, the ancient orator or new debater twice becomes the general equivalent through language: he projects tyranny or democracy in the more limited field of aesthetics or education. In both cases, his experiment reveals the general will on a small scale but in a tangible, visual, warm, physical fashion. He welcomes it, returns and transubstantiates it. In such a network of exchanges he acts like a beryl or an aquamarine in Verne's cavern. Sound waves or light rays, voices mimic looks. This is a small-scale model of a social network *in camera*.

Hands again express what is happening here better than eyes. The adult is holding the child whose hand caresses the father. Their attention is focused but moreover it fuses the bodies together. One single soul, one single body. This is society's first act.

A show in the Vichy theatre, Leonnard Leroux.

The multiple, the one and the Other

There are almost a thousand people here in front of me. Whom should I address? Everyone. I really see them, one by one, you the old man, you the adolescent, the brown or white-haired guy, the bald or hairy one, those with detached or well-meaning ears, bulging eyes, pretty girls, bespectacled men, lots of faces, chatting and frivolous. This panoptic amphitheatre is all eyes, wells of dangerous centres of attraction for the speaker.

No, that devouring monster that is either terrifying or standing up exalted and wonderfully benevolent, seems to me unique. Now they are sticking together, curdling and coagulating and form one compact mass, one single organism, one body and eye. The struggle is now one against one, it and me, between the two of us from the very first word. Love or battle? Will they stone me to death, cut me into pieces? Will they carry me on their shoulders (which would be the same thing)? Will that gaping hole absorb me?

Dispersed, they are all individuated. Together they are unified and concentrated and become one animal with a thousand heads. Two thousand eyes become one eye. One trench with several wells. They are often both at the same time; and sometimes through systole and diastole become commotions and eclipses, peristaltic movements, the waves' hollows and peaks, mountain tops and ocean tides, one after the other.

Miraculously however, a brilliant star or sun appears in this jumble. It turns out to be a masterpiece from a museum of fine arts. Suddenly in a rectangular frame with precise clear outlines, a face appears like an epiphany in a hole that has suddenly opened up as a precise geometric window, ecstatic as a Giotto figure, virginal as one of Fra Angelico's, or as clearly outlined as Carpaccio's; this face stands out while the other heads disappear and melt into the shadows. Emerging out of the blur, it becomes a signal amid the background noise, an apparition in the middle of the chaos. When painters draw halos around the heads of saints, all they do is emphasize their manifestation.

There are no longer thousands, but there is just one; and I only speak to you who appear before me as the archangel appeared before Mary, or Mary before the shepherdess Bernadette, or as the good apple that fell on Newton. You extricate yourself from the rest to manifest your essence which is framed, distinct, foreign and spreads around you what is called charisma: is it genius, thought, beauty? The hole is luminous and a well of potentialities. Into what depths will you plunge me?

The whole crowd sees me with this one haloed eye that I cherish seeing. I make love to the crowd that makes love to me.

Ecstatic, he sees the invisible. With his eyes or through his halo? Does it have access to what the gaze cannot see? Moreover, Fra Angelico has bored into his canvas a gaze inviting us also to see the invisible. This is the secret of painting.

Guido di Pietro called Fra Angelico, *Saint Cosmo's Face*, 1438-1446, convent of San Marco, Florence.

In this visit, the person on the left comes so close to the painting that she seems ready to go inside, while the young woman on the right has barely left the angelic framework, after having buttoned her blouse and handed Jesus over to Joseph.

Turner exhibit in Moscow, 2008; exhibit at the Fine Arts Museum in Dijon, 2003.

Painting

I see that face clearly framed, whose perfectly delineated outline suddenly opens a gap, an unexpected channel through which I can see her, and where she can perhaps see me, allowing me to perceive a whole other world.

In French an opening pierced in masonry for a basement or canalisation, an oven, sewer or a machine, is called a *regard*, a look. Most often such an opening has a casement closed off by a cover to facilitate visits or repairs, or at least inspections. This allows access to the trench, to the internal organs of the machine to repair possible defects and failures in the bowels that are generally not seen but which insure its continuous functioning. Is this access to the essential, to what is vital?

I have always thought that the power-that-be sitting on his throne hid with his ass the cover that closes off his view. The conditions of power remain forever concealed.

In a museum, the visitor walks along walls that are pierced by square or rectangular openings, the frames of the paintings. They are wells, trapdoors, skylights, windows, microscopes, telescopes and other scopes, through which we can see what we normally don't see because of our poor eyesight. Like a cover, my blindness closes off these openings. Lifting it up, I sometimes discover what there is to see through a microscope or telescope, through this opening.

Wrapped in skin, my body is closed off as by walls. Except that the skin is pierced by pores. Except that the eyes pierce the skin like ears, lips and nostrils. The eye is an opening in the sense of a window, a trapdoor or skylight. It has two eyelids as covers and is often covered up with wraps that prevent us from seeing.

Painters however have a visual perception that is the equivalent of an intellectual intuition or an ecstatic vision. Their paintings teach me how to open my eyelids and remove the covers.

Who will remove the covers from power?

Very different from angelic Paradise, this one places human silhouettes in the background and animals in the foreground of the garden. Anthropocentrism is forgotten and the world of flora and fauna preceding humans returns. The panther and the lion sit close to the goat and the horse in an earlier peace or after a struggle to survive. The peacock with a hundred eyes occupies the place of honor up front: it looks at us, we look at it and see the painting through its eyes. Is it wearing the eyes of the living beings around it? Does it offer an account for visitors draw to?

Jan Breughel 1, *Earthly Paradise*, oil on copper, 1621, Louvre Museum, Paris.

Sent
to see through
other eyes

We simply had windows before we looked through trenches, tunnels or wells
in the visible world; before we had spectacles, before all kinds of telescopes and
microscopes gave us images reproducing crystals and hidden organic tissues, the
swelling of the sea, the relief of the ocean bottom of the or giant galactic masses. We had
round portholes and square scuttles in boats.

Sitting comfortably in the lounge of the *Nautilus*, captain Nemo contemplated the marine species
parading along its mollusc-like submarine hull. The illustrations in *Twenty Thousand Leagues*
Under The Sea were like glances piercing the pages, like scuttles for the reader.

Reading comfortably in his study, like Nemo in his lounge, the reader saw the parade of octopuses
and crustaceans, sharks and cetaceans, and even a giant font where the hero cultivated his pearls in
utmost secrecy at the bottom of the Indian ocean. Similarly, Barbicane and Michel Ardan [characters
in Verne's *From the Earth to the Moon*] looking through the portholes of the *Columbiad*, saw the
stars and the corpse of Satellite, the dog that died upon take-off but remained attached to the
vehicle because of the attraction of its small gravitational force. I too used the illustrations that
pierced the pages of *From Earth to the Moon* as portholes. My grandmother used to tell me
my head was in the clouds from so much reading.

Instead of literally copying astronomical or ichthyological lists, which would be
deadly boring, Jules Verne created special envoys. He sent Nemo below the seas,
Barbicane into space and Arne Saknussem to the *Center of the Earth*, to
see what neither he nor anyone else could see. Come back and tell
us about it.

Nemo observes fish and mermaids through the porthole in
the lounge of the *Nautilus*; ours does not make a hole in the
hull of a submarine but in the frame of an illustration. Thanks
to this eye, common to both the captain and the reader, we
see an animal film in the ocean animated by a predecessor
of Cousteau: a subtle passage from literature to television.

Jules Verne, *Twenty Thousand Leagues Under the Sea*, chromo,
beginning of the 20th century.

Air, water, writing: those are excellent media whose delicacy makes it easy for messages and messengers to come through.

The Cyclops Polyphemus receives a letter brought by a messenger, detail of a fresco from Herculaneum, museo Archeologico Nazionale di Napoli.

Angelic messengers

Before him, Laplace also sent a god to find enough information to completely deduce the sequence of time. Hadamard, Duhem and Poincaré showed a century later that this all-seeing daemon could never achieve such certainty and thus opened up the reign of chaos and contingency. Ampère also sent his man to stick his feet in electric wires. Maxwell dispatched his daemon to a little window to count molecules invisible to the sender. When portholes and spectacles, and even the best performing telescopes and microscopes are no longer sufficient, curious people send envoys. Michel Strogoff, captain of the Tsar's couriers appears at the Kremlin: "Go to Siberia," the emperor orders him, "to see what the Tartars are doing and repair what they destroy!" Two journalists follow him.

Go under the seas, into space, go down the chimneys of volcanoes, have a look at the locked isolated enclosure of thermodynamic specialists. See what I cannot see and come back quickly to tell me about it.

Ulysses, go and sail in the Mediterranean Sea and return to Ithaca to see the portolan Penelope is weaving every day. Weep for your widowhood Andromache, and see all those die in plain sight, those whom you killed, impelled by duty to look back. Go to war, my lord Cid and come back to tell us about your killings. Harpagon, experiment with miserliness. Jacques, go travel with your master. Goriot, suffer as a father. Salammbo, explore Carthage. Don't these characters from books also act as delegates? There are other messengers among philosophers. Callicles, run violently, say Socrates and Plato. Zarathustra, go to Persia, says Nietzsche. It is impossible to cite the enormous number of characters delegated by Montaigne, whose pages swarm with such couriers, as do those of Pascal and Leibniz. The author sends them to see what he could never examine closely himself. He splits into two people so that the other as his lieutenant or placeholder will write as the author in his place.

My intelligent angels

All my characters fly swiftly like angels. I send them off and they return from their mission loaded with visions for my books. Many titles deserve their signature. It is time now for confessions. Yes, I live in a shadow where I may become stupid and blind. Panoptes, Hermes, Atlas, go seek intelligence and return, brilliant, to teach me what you have just seen. I stumble around in obscurity. Incandescent, plunge quickly into light and return home to share your enchantments. I flounder in archaic ignorance; you too, Thumbelina, go to the sciences and technologies and introduce me to your visions.

I call missions the tasks I give the troupe of my couriers. Their smooth and rapid mobility makes them so much more lucid and intelligent than I; and they are so much better educated and sophisticated; so much nicer, happier, cheerful and better surrounded with affection and love... that I beg them to write the best of my pages in my stead. Alone tonight, I write this page to give them a thousand thanks.

All pedestrians, cyclists and horsemen say: one eye on the next step and the other on the trip as a whole. We need to combine local precaution – where are we, what path are we taking? – with global precaution – from whence are we coming and where are we going? Before GPS or even the sextant, only angels had access to the second question and saw from above both the exodus from Egypt and the return to the Promised Land.

Nicolas Poussin, *La Fuite en Egypte*, 1657-1658, Louvre, Paris.

suffering
eyes

Lake Pavin

Seen from a helicopter or a plane, clear blue lake water lightens up the dark rocks and the dirty ice. Lakes also illuminate the face of the Alps, the Himalaya or the Massif Central in France. Immobile and ecstatic, they reflect the sky: lakes are the mountains' eyes.

One evening he left home with his backpack, broken-hearted by an impossible love. He took the train to Clermont and arrived there at night. Then he set out on foot for Lake Pavin. We will never know why he chose to go there. As far as we were able to ascertain, he arrived there two days later at break of dawn, dragging a fishing boat to the water's edge. Before embarking he had filled his bag with stones. He drifted towards the center of the perfect circumference where the volcano chimney curls down   toward the center of the Earth.

He remained in that deserted spot for a long time. Slowly he drew from his pocket the revolver he had just bought. He sat down on the side of the boat to tilt it so that the stones would pull him down under water, put the barrel of the gun in his mouth and without further thought pulled the trigger.

No, he did not fall into the lake. Early in the morning, a fisherman noticed something black in the grey fog, a boat motionless in the middle of the lake that appeared to be filled to the brim with water.

Two days later, the police called.

I have never been able to forget this scene: my brilliant friend departed on the silent waters of a vertiginous dead volcano. I was there once with a helpful friend, who in spite of my age held my hand. Did she know the danger I was in?

Since that daybreak, the lake's eye, filled with tears, looks at the sky, begging the living God to have mercy on a weak mortal.

The sky in a mountain lake looks bluer than above the clouds.
And so I see in your eyes a world more beautiful than banal reality.

The Cirque of Troumouse, National Park of the Pyrenees.

The Cyclops

Polyphemus Pangloss speaks every language to entice us. He is unmistakably seductive.

In his cavern, a cone-shaped well scattered with unmentionable remains and limbs of half-eaten corpses, his one clairvoyant eye sees the smallest details in the shadows, *perambulante in tenebris... [walking about in the shadows]* Insatiable he waits there to devour Ulysses and his sailors. In the back of his cavern, his eye and his mouth await us all.

Panoptic. The irresistible force of the black hole of Evil swallows everything that happens and fails to happen, the material and immaterial, red and blue, high and low, reputable and disreputable. In a middling high and unstable equilibrium, Good continuously loses followers. The lowest of low, the evil eye retrieves the remains, ripe fruit, dead leaves and swallows them. The Cyclops feeds on them. As the harsh and repulsive prince of the world, Evil applies without exception the necessary law Newton scattered over the span of the entire Universe. A fixed point of attraction and a source of potentialities, he reigns secure in the depth of depths. Exceedingly unusual, exceptional, extremely fragile, tremendously weak, infinitely gentle, Good flies in rare and unstable weightlessness.

Strange: even though living on seismic soil and on islands half destroyed by eruptions, the ancient Greeks had no word for volcano. This may be so, but like the Latin god residing under Etna, don't the Cyclopses with their single eye who also lived in subterranean caverns, don't they visibly embody the magmatic chambers and the round crater? Characters often say more and better than a concept.

Jules Romain, *La Chute des Titans*, detail, 1525-1535, Museo civico di Palazzo Te, Camera dei Giganti, Mantua.

Porthole eyes

The scene takes place aboard the 35,000-ton battleship *Richelieu*. In the fifties it was docked at a quay in Brest as a training ship. After exams and competitions, young midshipmen would be sent here and there on the world's seas. The initiation rite for the new class was to pierce the ship's steel hull. As a supreme honor on the last day, the admiral invited two or three little male chicks representing the brood to his table.

I was one of them. Our shoes were clean, uniform pants perfectly creased, new caps on our heads; we dined in the admiral's quarters on the main deck, sitting up straight with polished smiles on our faces.

"Hey there, midshipman," from the head of the table the master yelled at me, sitting at the other end, "I was told bad things about you."

– Too honored, admiral.

– You dabble in philosophy.

– True, admiral.

– Have you ever thought about the problem of Evil?

– Often, admiral.

– Do you believe in the demon, the devil, Satan?

– Yes, admiral.

– Do you have any real reason to believe in it?

– I do, admiral.

– What, how and when?

– Very often, and even this very morning, admiral.

– I order you to show us.

– Yes, admiral."

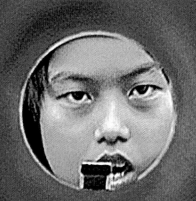

I get up from the table, cross the room, move to a porthole hidden by a dark blue curtain with the battleship's seal, slide the cloth hanging from the golden rod aside and open the cover. Under the lavender sky of the Brest Spring, there are two 380 turrets, whose two times four cannons point up obliquely for eventual shots beyond the horizon.

"Here it is admiral."

Never have I admired these Navy officers more, their culture, their superb intelligence and their wisdom. All looked silently at those big organs of God's thunder and the meal resumed after a few meditative minutes. They knew about violence better than I and they were judging the self-importance of a petulant wise guy. I was not punished for my arrogance and I am ashamed today to tell a story that is more evidence of an adolescent desire to show off than of some kind of courage.

I had to write *La Guerre mondiale* to finally understand the role played by the police and the army in the dense, banal and hidden distribution of human violence. Unlike many others, I have required much time to mature.

However, for a long time I have reflected on what I could not see through the porthole: heaps of bloody flesh and dying screams at the other end of those long tubes resembling telescopes, aimed at worsening the miserable human condition.

The admiral orders me: "Midshipman, go and see death and come back to change my point of view." "Yes, sir" says the philosopher. He goes back to port and returns from Lake Pavin, whose eye cries to the sky.

If pilots releasing bombs from very high up, if fighters gunning from a distance, if they were to aim at their wives' faces, would they pull the trigger? If your child were put in the place of the target, would you shoot? If instead of the rape victim or dismembered bodies, your parents appeared, would you photograph violent scenes? Each victim is your sister.

Agartala, State of Tripura, India, January 8, 2006.

rejoicing
eyes

My gaze finds joy in the joy that your gaze finds in the joy I experience seeing you.

Only love can keep perpetual motion going.

As a uniquely gratuitous production, knowledge, like love,

emerges from the same perpetual motion between the world and us,

between two subjects and two gazes.

a

other's

eyes

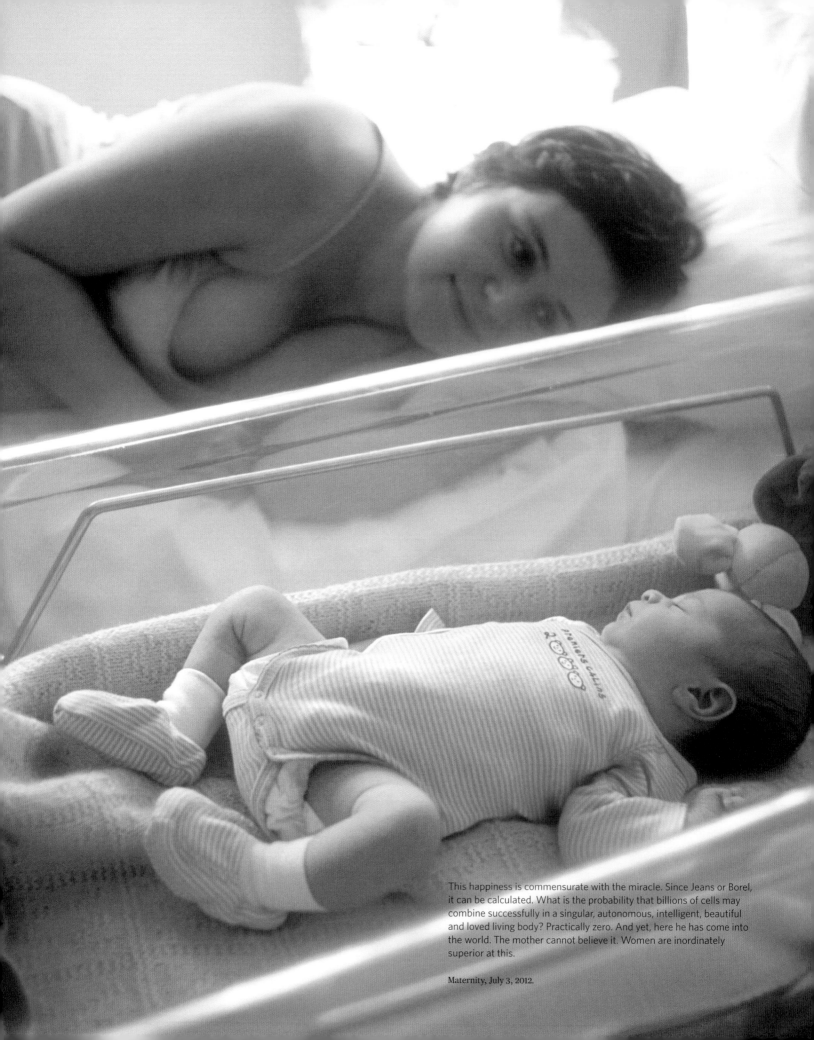

This happiness is commensurate with the miracle. Since Jeans or Borel, it can be calculated. What is the probability that billions of cells may combine successfully in a singular, autonomous, intelligent, beautiful and loved living body? Practically zero. And yet, here he has come into the world. The mother cannot believe it. Women are inordinately superior at this.

Maternity, July 3, 2012.

After labor

People considered her ugly, as if a young and intelligent woman could be without charm. I had known her as a sincere but rather plain friend for a long time. One morning I was told she had been delivered of a baby boy. Without heeding what day or time it was, I ran to the florist and then to the maternity ward where I arrived impromptu like an oaf. The month of April was spreading dirty grey soot and a dull icy glimmer as happens sometimes in the mountains in spring at the bitter tail end of winter.

As I enter, a strange light floods me as if a dense, tangible and unknown dawn were shining down on me, like a shower streaming down my body. The bed with the white sheets, the blue crib surrounded by lace, the pink new-born baby, his eyes closed, the calm silent room dotted with yellow spots... all pointed to the end of labor pains now that everything was bathed in light.

She opens her eyes and suddenly I, the sterile male, suddenly see from where gushes forth, originates, wells up, explodes the vital impulse of happiness and the origin of beauty. I see her hair ringed with a shiny halo I will never have.

This middle-class pornography gives us insight into the Belle Epoque. To wrap the serpent around the papier-mâché tree, the director had to borrow a fireman's hose. With a falsely timid smile, the chubby silly goose gets ready to succumb to a naughty temptation.

Eve and the Serpent, erotic postcard, c. 1900.

I remembered then our common mother Eve and the serpent. Amidst the dry yellow fall grass, a reptile – what kind, since there are so many here? – looks intently at a blue jay. Erect, with bowed head, immobile, intense, eyeball to eyeball, the reptile stares at the bird. Feathers twitching, the latter blinks, stumbles, loses its balance and falls. For the first time I witness a scene of hypnotism. I come closer softly so as not to interrupt the fascinating spectacle.

I face the following problem: if I make a noise by moving and awaken the jay from its fatal ecstasy, it flies away; I save its life, but I deprive the rattlesnake of its prey. If on the contrary I let the situation continue, I favor the reptile but contribute to the bird's death. In both cases there is life and death. It is the law of the jungle, to eat or be eaten, to kill in order to survive. Avoiding death, defending oneself and starving others, again this too means killing. In both cases, there is death. I make a decision and I clap. The jay leaves and streaks away, no bird this time. Another anamnesis.

No, I am no longer walking on the hill facing the campus. I stand in reminiscent rapture stock-still in the first garden of Eden, the paradise in Mesopotamia. My name is Eve. Motionless in the presence of the serpent – which kind, there are so many here – she witnesses a similar scene. The serpent will devour the bird or starve to death. Death, and death again is before her, even as she thinks she is immortal.

Our mother's purity

Eat or be eaten, perish no matter what. Eve, who is just, considers the law of the jungle abhorrent. This is the decisive revelation, the emergence of a sublime intuition that creates the human species. From the beginning Eve declares that the violence of flesh against flesh is original sin. Animals like me had never become aware of this. She discovers the law and finds it unjust. She wants no part in this tragedy. She decides to leave.

With this immemorial act, Eve invents *Homo Sapiens* and its history by freeing it from animal, paradisiacal "natural" unconsciousness. She starts the human era in the sense of science, consciousness and knowledge, and also creates humanity in the sense of goodness, wisdom and charm. As a result of her intuition and her merciful decision, we no longer have to live like the jay or the serpent, chirping or hissing, but we speak of forgiveness. We become more human as we disobey the atrocious law of the jungle, kill or die, which is both "nature's" violence and original sin.

I clap and the serpent disappears in the yellow grass. I wake up and leave the Garden of Eden; I return to the California sky. Now however, I understand the miracle wrought by our common ancestor; I see her as virginal, the mother of the knowledge of good and evil, who is charged with original sin for having recognized it from the beginning. Did she steal a piece of fruit from the apple tree of knowledge? Did she joyfully steal in the ecstasy of knowing?

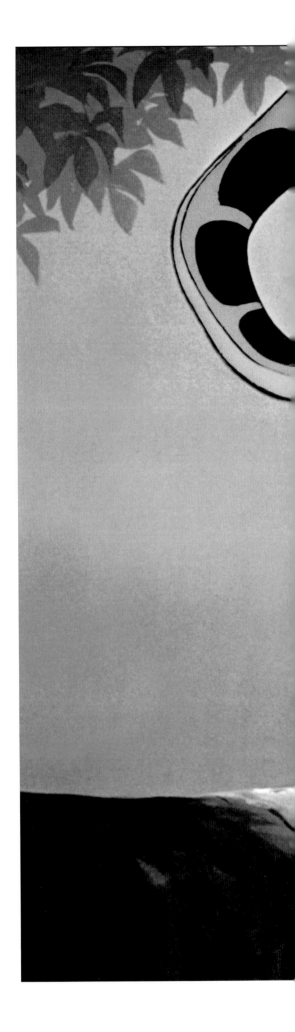

When our art teacher tried to make us understand how not to draw, he invariably gave us the example of a Walt Disney cartoon. Since then, the consumer culture from the United States has submerged the world. We no longer can tell why such a horror is ugly. O memory of Kipling!

Walt Disney, *The Jungle Book*, 1967.

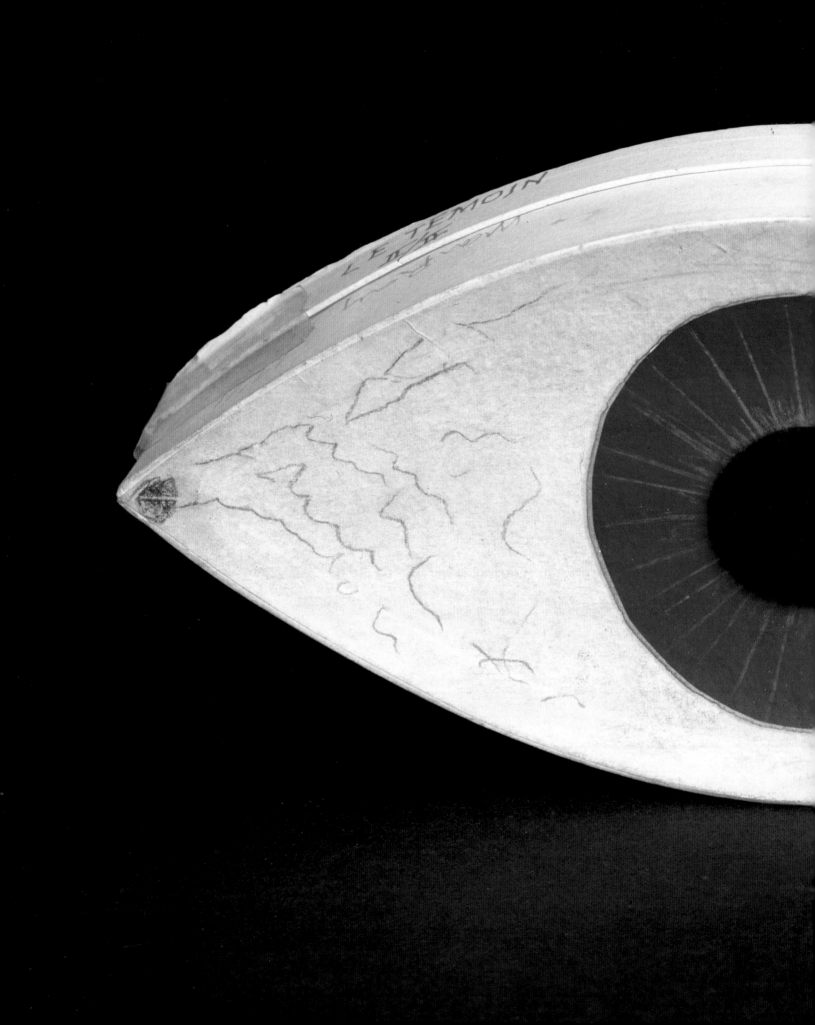

head

eyes

The hairdresser and the mechanic

Once upon a time, there was intelligent television. In those prehistoric beginnings, subtle directors dreamt of sharing knowledge. One fine evening, one of them gathered together a Nobel prize-worthy biologist, an astronomer who later became a popularizing celebrity, in short, a small team of bespectacled knowalles. I was one of them. The show put us opposite another team composed of workers and artisans selected because they had never gone beyond fifth grade. The hairdresser had glorious blonde hair and the mechanic swayed his formidable shoulders...

This fine company was to ask us to explain clearly something they had never understood. The astronomer spun around spiralling galaxies and the biologist pivoted twisting DNA. We were all dazzled, myself included. When it was my turn, the hairdresser challenged me to define the infinite. She said it was impossible to understand; you cannot go where numbers go so fast that you can neither count nor see them.

"Don't run away so far," I told her, "Stay with me. Count to ten, that should be enough. Here are ten numbers, right? However, if you only take the even numbers, 2, 4, 6, 8, 10, there are only five. Five is smaller than ten.

– That is too easy, said the blonde.

– You are making fun of us, said the big guy.

– Let us go further. Lay out all the numbers until you have had enough, until you can no longer see or count them.

– There are so many, said the blonde.

– Too many, added the mechanic

– Let us make an effort. Under each number of this huge list, place its double: under 1, set 2, under 3, 6, and so on. There are just as many because for each upper number there is an even number below it; however, below there are fewer because there are no uneven numbers there.

– My God, exclaimed the blonde.

– Are you messing around with us? The mechanic complained.

– No Sir, I am sincere, believe me, but this is truly the infinite.

– Aha, the glorious blonde cried out, with her lower-class accent, the infinite then is when there is as much above and below, so when the half is the equivalent of the total? (she was opening and closing her hands as if she were ruffling someone's hair to inspect it) So this is how we can understand the infinite, bravo!

– Bingo, I get it", exclaimed the mechanic and stretching out his trembling hands towards the blonde as if explaining to her, "there is so much that if you went down into some well, there would be as much in a third, in a tenth, in a hundredth as in the totality, you see that dear, in that well?"

He was practically love struck.

The television audience was delighted!

"Well....", the blonde coolly resumed, looking at me mockingly, "the fact that any part is the equivalent of the whole, does not get me very far. You replace the dizzying horizontal progression without possible interruption, with a vertical dizzying fall into the abyss; whether we deal with a faraway distance or a well, big deal!"

The scenery has changed and reversed; I thought the studio lights were burning. She saw in my popping eyes that I was beginning to understand what my scholarly naïveté had failed to discover. Around the platform, a harsh light illuminated the cameras and fell on me.

I rushed to kiss Mrs. Glorious Blonde's both hands, to thank her for having shared with me her blessedly intelligent intuition, I no longer thought of myself as particularly advanced.

The joyous mystery of Klein's work resides in the fact that his models were women walking nude in his atelier; he ended up painting huge monochromatic blues. Can the visitor perceive beautiful strolling ladies hiding in these canvasses?

New York, Museum of Modern Art, 2007.

I must have been almost eight years old. The declaration of war and general mobilization had thinned the ranks of teachers. Given the shortage, all the classes had to be merged. At the end of a longish recess, I was sent to another class. Going from the fifth grade to the ninth meant joining the big kids. They had golf pants, while I had short pants; they already played rugby while I played jai alai. They had several teachers while I had only one all day.

I see standing in front of the blackboard an elderly man. He is at least forty years old, discharged, lame, nice. He writes quickly with chalk: x-2=0. What the...? Another language? I understand 0 and 2, but what is this x, where is this coming from? I can tell that the teacher is using it to count. Impossible! Can we really mix letters and numbers? Can we count with y's and z's and turn the alphabet around?

A few words from the old fellow, and the light of abstraction begins to shine in my head: I see, I understand, I know! X is a piggy bank where you can throw all the numbers you want. I get it. Of course, he plays with the piggy bank without having to know how much money it contains. And he has the right to do so... also, it is easier and goes further. I have never lost this piggy bank, which makes me feel prodigiously rich with a horn of plenty, and I have remained utterly bedazzled. Ecstatic, I entered an enchanted palace, far from the labor involving pickaxes and spades in the fields or on the banks of the Garonne, but especially far from the war and the screams of hate. As I changed my habits, by squinting, by talking, by listening, by touching and by feeling differently, I discovered the real island of intelligence. I understood that cost and saling prices, train schedules and faucets, supposedly so

Low extraction and high abstraction

concrete, hid the calculations of station platforms, sordid grocery stores or blocked drains. The x's of that kind old man with his silver spectacles invited me into the miraculous paradise of understanding. Finally! I suddenly decided then that if possible I would never leave this place of light where the real is illuminated by the universal eye.

During the recess that followed I was flying. I thought I saw the playground full of flowers and sunlight, lilacs and primroses. I wore my sateen pinafore, usually dirty and covered with crumbs and mud, as if it were the organdie dress I had seen on my beautiful sister on her wedding days. Gaining a few sizes, I glimpsed a joyful, bright life in the future.

It is still shining with that unseen vision.

Years or centuries later, after that wonderful day, I learned about what Leibniz had called *cogitatio caeca*. He applied these words to blind intuition; a vision of what one cannot see, a formal thought independent of its content. Just as I rarely remember the money I put in that piggy bank, no one knows or will ever know which numbers the letters x, y and z indicate. Nevertheless, it is so easy to calculate with them that algebra's efficiency can be summed up in the oxymoron, to know with the help of unknowns. You don't even have to make a hole in the piggy bank. Darkness gives light. Choose the shadows over prey, which will be returned to you a hundredfold.

The painter sees what seeing people, who are actually blind, do not know how to see. One of these lucid people invented painting to show the kingdom of the blind the sensible substance of the world, the gazes of the Universe. They enter visual sensation like the great inventors enter unexpected intuitions, often blindly, or like mystics in the dark night leading to ecstasy and contemplation. They break the gazes' covers or sometimes even see without removing them.

Blind marvels

Inspired by Mondrian's paintings, Yves Saint Laurent designed twenty unforgettable dresses. Leibniz thought that the words *white* and *blue* had the same root as *blazon*, the shield that came from a skin, and *blesser* (French for *wounded*) or *blasée* (French for *dulled*) by alcohol. The association of the painter and the designer gave new life to this crazy hypothesis, where color joins the support and again, the veil the painting.

Piet Mondrian, *Composition in Blue and White*, 1936, Museum of Art, Düsseldorf.

Mirroring neurons

To see a gesture many times allows one to perform it fast, especially if an admired body does it perfectly. The young people of Agen [a rugby center] never learned how to play rugby; it is useless to teach soccer to the children of Saint-Etienne [a football center]; Johann Sebastian suckled chorale at the breast of the Bach family. There was no question of innate gifts but constant viewing led to the acquisition of a refined practice, a family practice in one case, cultural or urban habits in other cases. We now know that sensory nervous conduits stimulate motor muscles, even when the spectator does not move. To see is to do. The virtual gesture precedes and teaches the actual one. By digging into one's head, one learns how to dig head first. It was inevitable that those mirror neurons were discovered in Italy, the blessed home of the *commedia dell'arte* and *opera seria*. Mimicry on the stage and among the spectators.

Let us imitate one another and the group will cohere. Do these active neurons shape and glue together society as a whole? Is theatre the site that forms the collectivity? Is "entertainment society" a pleonasm? Do we live together to enjoy seeing ourselves and to love each other? Is the so-called collective intelligence reduced to repetitiveness, to a network of crossings where a thousand bright rays send each other rigid identical images, reflected by mirrors whose facets overlap and construct political animals? Do similar people meet because they resemble each other or does meeting produce similar people? Does society simply reproduce itself?

It is not the world we see at first, but each other. Are we envious and jealous mimics? The so-called humanities and social sciences very much preceded – and I mean by millions of years – the objective sciences. To wit, most Greek scholars were put on trial, accused of the horrible crime of observing the sky rather than taking care of the city's business. Before the tribunal, a jury of political sociologists condemned physics, astronomy and medicine. Same under Stalin and Althusser.

182

Shaping or destroying the icon

Another battle. In 1929, when René Magritte showed his painting *Trahison des images*, adorned with the sentence "This is not a pipe," he revived an old debate opposing iconoclasts and iconophiles in Byzantium around 730. The debate itself renewed the archaic question of abstraction which has been asked since the beginnings of geometry. The destroyers of images said that the divine could not be represented and they were right. The icon lovers said that images were not the divine but helped to venerate it, and they were right. As usual, the big pointless fights that supposedly make history favor the pugnacious and destructive side rather than reason, which is rather pacific. Similarly, the triangle I trace on the sand is nothing like the one I use for my proof, but how can I reason easily without this drawing? Hundreds of teachers are still debating whether it is better to talk about apples or faucets before taking about points, lines and numbers.

Preferring geometry and logic to images, the great exclusive monotheisms – Judaism, Islam, and some Protestant denominations – side with the iconoclasts. Catholics and Orthodox religions are more anthropological and pluralist and ceaselessly reproduce icons. We moderns love so-called abstract painting and so side with the former, without being aware of it.

However, the invasion of photography and later cinema, television and cell phones, newspapers and manuals with text-effacing illustrations, and advertising posters, has provoked a torrential tsunami of images. They flood the world, roads and streets, public places, private homes, schools and eyes. To preserve its originality, painting has found refuge in the austere bosom of the iconoclasts.

This image beautifully shows the trouble with some stairs. In general, the eyes easily adapt to the moving process required to descend. Here suddenly there is a time lag between vision and movement: *vertigo!* Belonging to the same family as *vertical* and *vertebra*, the word refers to a common root, the preposition *vers* (French for *towards*) indicating a transferring movement: to go towards but also a rotation: *vertere*, in Latin, means to turn. These stairs that descend vertically and turn, give vertigo to my vertebrae!

Sam Berger aka Sam Szafran, *Untitled*, oil pastel, 1981, musée d'Art moderne, Paris.

The poverty of images

Abstraction prevailed. With my own eyes I saw a brilliant blind man. He passed the entrance exam to *l'Ecole normale*, signed up for literature, suddenly branched off into Mathematics, graduated with the *Agrégation* and then also obtained a doctorate. None of those with eyesight, or anyone in my class could have accomplished such a feat of intelligence and abstraction. It would have been even more impossible for deaf and dumb people who have learning difficulties since early childhood. Other blind people such as cathedral organists excel in music and are sometimes composers, like the great Louis Verne. Homer wrote the *Iliad* and *the Odyssey;* Milton, *Paradise Lost.* Contrary to what fashion and the icon tell us, images give less information than sound. Even though the eye is lavishly connected to the back of the skull and so sends its ramifications throughout the entire brain, it is relatively weak and teaches less than the ear, which is much stronger than is thought. The radio is more satisfying to listeners than the television is to viewers. The relationship between the image and what the news is saying remains vague and sometimes turns into comical nonsense. Even with sumptuous colors and shapes, films without a script quickly become trashy. Textbooks are full of images that are nevertheless a thousand times less effective than the text. Don't be surprised if children don't learn much. Cover your ears and you run a greater risk than closing your eyes. Bits and beeps trump pixels.

In order for plentiful information to emerge continuously from the image as from a horn of plenty, rare and real geniuses are needed such as Raphael, Poussin and Soulages: they paint eyes. Not an image, but a gaze.

The day when players score more soccer goals and fewer baskets, it would again be worth watching those two games. Here the players do not look at the adversary or the basket, but both stare intensely at the coveted ball. This proves that their opposition goes through that marvelous object whose path marks their relations by separating or joining the teams.

Michigan-Indiana encounter, 2014.

The birth of humankind

I was not yet fifteen years old and the World War had just ended. In my native Aquitaine, there was some vague talk about Father Breuil and the caves of Lascaux. We had no inkling of prehistory. On a bicycle trip to see friends not far from the Perigueux, I asked about going to visit them. With my brother who made fun of my curiosity, I went into a cave not yet crowded with curious people. I think that in some halls I was the only one. Fascinated, I stayed a long time. I doubt if I have ever felt a religious or almost mystical presence so intensely. It was not because I had gone underground in the dark with weakly glimmering shadows that I was taken out of the world, but because those reddish drawings with their black and sometimes partial lines pierced the rock and opened up a look into a distant elsewhere. No, I did not imagine going back into the past to become a caveman. On the contrary, looking at the heads and the bodies, I foresaw openings, excavations, multiple original tunnels that all pointed towards a sublime future where humanity, reconciled with itself and with animals, entered an Eden of fabulous knowledge, ecstasy and love. I never found out whether those drawings were done by the very first painter; I never believed those condescending legends about the hunt and magic. What I learned there and then, as one of the sons and descendants, is that artistic creation always augurs a new humanity. The ancestral genius of Lascaux was inspired to write and name animals, just like Adam, and just like God, created man, and so created me. This paradise, far from residing in the morbid memory of wars and a lost happy past, was projected onto a space to be constructed with our esthetic, cognitive, practical and creative brush. I left this cathedral empowered.

Like the artist, the philosopher anticipates. What is the meaning of this beginning, this initial vision?
Da capo [back to the beginning]: half a century later, scholarly friends allowed me to return to Lascaux, this time through a virtual door in a southern suburb of Paris. At Dassault Systèmes, a company specializing in computer graphics and aircraft design, engineers lead you into in a laboratory cave, and require you to put on felt shoes and special glasses. I was overwhelmed to see there the sanctuary that had delighted my youth and I understood again that Plato's cave, far from criticizing the prisoners, on the contrary, celebrates the inventors of writing, of painting and representation. I had returned to the original site of that discovery at the very moment of our time when other ways of seeing were invented. As I said in the beginning of my book: when ways of seeing change, one revisits the origin of vision. Looks converged on my reality from those virtual animals dancing on virtual walls. Did they bring it to life, did they reinforce it?

This is not a face or an eye or a balloon, but the ecstasy when you see the sky seeing you.
René Magritte, *Les Belles Relations*, 1967, private collection.

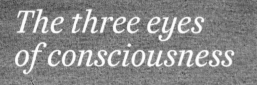

The three eyes
of consciousness

Since then I have understood that we humans have three eyes. First, there is one that
reflects light; this we have in common with emeralds and rubies that flash in Verne's cave and that
perceive what is useful or desirable. We have that one in common with sunflowers, maple leaves,
carp, cows and rattlesnakes. Then there is the eye that distinguishes at a distance the truth or falsity
of appearances, their delightful or repulsive traits; it also discerns amidst the glimmers the why of
this truth or that falsehood. It understands what constitutes lovability or indifference; we share
this in some respects with some of our primate cousins.
Then finally there is the limitless eye that from beyond an infinite
limit perceives the x in my old classroom,
my blonde's infinite and the
abstract

universal
of knowledge:
science, and its ethical conduct.
In humans, these three eyes see at the same
time and interact while each feeds the perception of the
two others. It is difficult to see things as they are in the here and the
now, without the judging and partisan second eye intervening and sometimes
preferring the improbable or the less attractive; the third eye sees the universal. Does this interaction lead to consciousness or does it emerge from consciousness? In any case, it reveals the world.
Some paint God's eye in a triangle. I redraw it like our eye, one single eye with three functions and
as in the three persons, the ternary form turning on itself. In short, we see this or that now, its causes
or beginning, but we also see it as if we had always seen them for centuries and centuries.
Do I draw the Trinitarian eyes of the Holy Spirit?

No gaze emerges from any point in this space. From each site a light rod emerges. This is how the painter sees God's ubiquity: he is everywhere, and from everywhere he sees everything.

Verrocchio, *the Baptism of Christ*, c. 1475, Galleria degli Uffizi, Florence.

fire
of
eyes,

fire
of
god

192

God's gaze

We see only the profile of
things depending on the angle they present to
us. After the Renaissance invented perspective, our
classical authors, as I mentioned, used the term of perspectival
representation for this conception as if the idea was to engrave a scene
from a certain angle. The painter, draftsman and architect can draw from such
a model as many profiles or perspectival representations as they wish, an almost
infinite number because of the proliferation of angles from which they can imagine or
design the model.

When infinitesimal calculus was invented, some philosophers got the idea of gathering all the
profiles in one image, which if it were possible at all, would be the integral or the sum of such
an infinity. Leibniz called it the geometral of the object or sometimes its ichnography. Since the
omnipresent God occupies each position, his perception of a given object is exactly such an
ichnography, the sum of profiles. He is possibly the only One who sees things correctly. Only He
knows the global truth. We can only see oblique projections.

We are limited to perspectives. And so all the world's drawings, portraits and paintings just show
profiles relative to the position of our view. The artist would have to identify with God to realize
an ichnography whose representation would yield the integral knowledge of things, in short
their truth. However, the latter remains inaccessible.

He can go crazy in the attempt to find that limit. Again, this is a story told by Balzac
in T*he Unknown Masterpiece.* Unable to attain that truthful perfection, the
painter Frenhofer, in his delirium, produced a painting in which he thought
he had hidden it. However, instead of an integral, it only showed an
indescribable chaos of shades, forms and colors, whose
jumble preceded God's creative gesture. Hence the
painting's name, *La Belle Noiseuse.*

We think of chaos as pure disorder. Here, to the contrary, a perfect
organization transforms it into a sun and a gaze. If God had found the
jumble looking like this, He would have had nothing to do. Associating the
eye with a nebula is a fabulous idea: in front, information! *Magnum chaos,* inlaid woodwork by Giovan Francesco Capoferri, after a drawing by Lorenzo Lotto, detail, 16th century; Basilica Santa Maria Maggiore, Bergamo.

At first "noise" signified sound and fury, noise in English and rage in French. No, the painter is not delirious.

On the contrary, he and Balzac understood what is at stake in representation and the infinite classical difference between multiple perspectival representations and a unique ichnography. The proof is that in the middle of the painting's crazy smears, the artist has drawn a bare, delicious foot, perfectly formed and colored. ιχνοσ, *ichnos*. In Greek the word indeed designates a foot or footstep. That is pre-

cisely the signature of the mas-
the master of all possible
By the way, how would this
eyes that, infinitely removed
intregral or geometral, in
and Balzac show that very
ground noise. When the con-
hear the residual fluctuation of

terpiece, so named because it is
pieces.
ichnography appear to our
from God, will never see the
short, the truth? Frenhofer
painting: it resembles back-
duit delivers no message, we
atoms whose Brownian motion

vibrates in the matter that filament is made of. Whether the sea is calm, agitated or stormy, one can hear the same murmur, which is all that it can produce, now, in the past, or forever. The known Universe with its profusion of galaxies breathes in the same way. Every crowd produces this brouhaha and hurly burly. Genesis tells us that this is the chaos out of which God kneaded, fashioned and separated His raw material.

Does creation imply pre-formation? Saturated with angelic *homunculi*, Eve's uterus, round like an eye, contents all future living beings. A fractal, this round barrel or original bank encloses a box of boxes of boxes, century after century. Will the character with the pleated robe inseminate the ovules?

Jean Colombe, *Création du monde par Dieu*, in *Heures de Louis de Laval*, 15th century, BNF, Paris.

Comme au second jour dieu fist le firmament ent
de ly eaues et divisa les eaues celles qui estoient
soubz le firmamt des eaues qui estoict sur le firma
ment<del> nõma le firmamt ael. Ge̅s ij° ca</del>

Background noise

In the beginning, after the big bang the divine creator was faced with background noise. Since we do not see the One, chaos remains our destiny. We are notthe one and we navigate amidst disturbances. My thought, my flesh, my cry, my sentences and my tears bathe in the divine or worldly raw material: this is the hurly burly. I left classical mathematics behind and the Leibnizian dream of understanding how God created the world. I then spent my life completely immersed in background noise, swallowed up and absorbed by it, attentive to its murmur, fluctuations, and the signals emerging from its multiplicity. I was in love with dripping and troublesome creatures rising up from the sea, just as Ulysses saw Nausicaa surface. I have tried to draw all this as combined kaleidoscopes, to paint what coalesced, to multiply the enormous fluctuating range of possibilities generating contingent existences and their first emerging steps. Finally, I attempted to sketch the integral of colors in white: to discover how colorful Harlequin suddenly became the lunar Pierrot dressed in incandescent white.

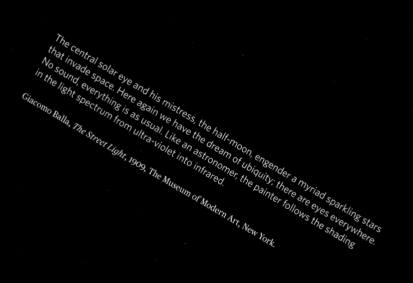

The central solar eye and his mistress, the half-moon, engender a myriad sparkling stars that invade space. Here again we have the dream of ubiquity: there are eyes everywhere. No sound, everything is as usual. Like an astronomer, the painter follows the shading in the light spectrum from ultra-violet into infrared.

Giacomo Balla, *The Street Light*, 1909, The Museum of Modern Art, New York.

Fire
in the ice
corridor

At the refuge we rise at 2:00 o'clock: under
the stars, deep darkness. We have some weak
tea. We leave at 3, tightly roped-up together,
scantily-lit by a helmet lamp whose thin beam
draws vague profiles of ice and rocks. There are
difficult passages on the long approach along the
glacier ridges that are the more easily crossed as
our partial blindness makes us oblivious to the surrounding danger. Our ice axes and crampons hooked
in, we start the slow vertical ascent of the ice corridor in
front of us.

Suddenly, like a bomb, daybreak falls along this whole
pocket. White like dawn, it explodes in the dark night, slides
on the translucent crystal and changes the dirty white into a
half cylinder of pure light. The empty space is entirely saturated
with incandescent and multi-colored fire. My hands are gone and I
no longer have a body, human flesh or a head. Have I entered the
source of my lamp? I have become just a tiny eye in the eyeball of a large
eye, not knowing whether they receive or emit light. I am steeped in light,
transformed into transparency, transcending into dazzling brilliance,
transported weightlessly, transubstantiated into what must be divinity.
Deum de Deo, lumen de lumine, God of God, light of light.

To him, who guided me for almost three
decades, to her who accompanied me
in those climbing expeditions, I dedicate
my admiration, gratitude and love.
I can never thank them enough for the
joys we shared.

Ice corridor in the Mendenhall glacier, Alaska,
2008.

Experts continue to discuss the validity of the evidence concerning levitation. The levitations of Saint Theresa of Avila for instance, seem credible. Whatever the physical reality of these ecstasies, Simone Weil, in her famous book, opposed *Gravity and Grace*, as if the latter were an exception to a universal law.

Giovanni Lanfranco, *Maria Magdalene raised by angels*, 1640, Museo nazionale di Capodimonte, Naples.

Rapture

In the
Provence
region, among
the various sta-
tues that make up
the Christmas Nativity
scene, there is the Ravi,
stiffer than the other figures. A
naïve outsider and observer, he is
barely part of the scene as he was just
passing by, like any of us. Suddenly pinned
to the ground by what he sees, he is dumb-
founded, astonished and petrified; immobile and
stock-still he is transported to the third heaven and
becomes a part of the holy scene. Like everyone else, he
has his feet on earth and his head in the divine.
His gesture is so vibrant that an obviously motionless statue seems
to move. Life is stabilized as it settles down while the stone, deviating
from equilibrium, finds a dynamic. This is the double paradox of a living
movement that stops and an inert stillness that leaps up, of an organism that
sleeps or dies and of raw material that wakes up or revives. Descriptions or figures
of speech are insufficient to understand that situation. It is not enough to read in the
word "ecstasy" the immobile statuary and the act that liberates it. Yes, rapture
immobilizes and transports.

In mysticism lies the secret of sculpture as a source of religion and the reason for its sometimes
captivating beauty. Ecstasy makes it possible for either the body or the mind to fly but adds tons to
the body it enraptures. Mary Magdalene of Pazzi went to the top moldings with light steps but became
so heavy that ten strong people were unable to move her. Bernini sculpted Saint Theresa in ecstasy, ethereal
and compact.

In mysticism lies the secret of painting as a source of reason and religion and of its sometimes captivating beauty. Ecstatic vision enraptures the view and its light floods the world, both the person who sees and is seen by the world. The whole scene thus illuminated is bathed in the molten gold of the halo. The colors and forms, things and humans together become what they are. Everything sees. Thanks to Fra Angelico, the Virgin and Gabriel see me through the limbus of the halo and show me the invisible they see.

No matter how deep my own thoughts or those I shared with other people, whatever intoxication I experienced from discoveries or inventions, however musical my sentences, no matter how many beautiful creations I have contemplated, however perfect some happiness has seemed, a supreme intuition told me those events were like islands for sailors. I knew that while they were rare and might not happen at all, underneath there is a stand, a base, a continuous support like some quiet and soft security where beauty is always present and is the other name for the light of intelligence and joy.

Some wiser than I have called the overabundant continent I see and where I sometimes live, God, Being, heaven, truth or philosophy. However they have always said that this other world is merged with ours, that it is the profound and simple reality of things. Angels, envoys, and messengers whisked them away without their feet touching the ground, which proves that there is no road or method to get there. Archangels and cherubim accompanied them to show them the layout and the towers. They are so happy there that, on their return, they consider themselves emigrants or nomads as they wander in the ordinary earthly valley, to which they were obliged to go home at some point; they wonder what they are doing there.

During a take-off in Montreal in the winter, my plane seemed to enter a boreal dawn. It had little color, milky white, and floated like a scarf on the earth's head to protect it from the cold or like some mystical bedazzlement to counteract Evil.

Aurora Borealis, Kvaløy, Norway.

No matter how deep their thoughts have been, whatever rapture some work has given them, how beautiful some rare pages seemed, they know they remain pieces of flotsam from some wreck of a voyage. Any trip here on earth, whether mobile or immobile, is only a preliminary preparation for a new departure on the wings of angels towards the space of their hopes.
They are naïve and appalled, delighted, elated by what happens in the world.

"If the soul were capable of knowing God without the world, the world would not have been created for it. The world was created for the soul so that the soul's eye would work to strengthen itself to bear the divine light. The Sun's brilliance does not fall on the Earth without having first been thinned out in the air and shone on other things because otherwise man's eye could not bear it. The divine light is so powerful and so bright that our soul's eye could not bear it if our look were not strengthened by matter, raised by images, directed towards the divine light and progressively accustomed to it."

Maître Eckhart, Sermon 32, in *Traités et sermons*, trad. and introduction
Alain de Libera, Flammarion, coll. «GF Philosophie», 1993, p. 333-334

Christ in the Parthenon

Disguised under the label of tourism, the Third World War is covering the most beautiful sites in the world with shit, vendors and hideous noises. For once, here is some truth in advertising: never visit Machu Picchu, or the pyramids of Egypt, or Ayers Rock in the center of Australia; don't climb Mont Blanc, don't go to Mount Everest or the Cote d'Azur. The rotten evil of the irresistible drift towards cheap junk has dirtied and degraded everything to the point of hiding all beauty. Mystical in the past, the nicest sites in the world now tragically look like the hideous access zones of our cities. Try and find anywhere the simple discrete beauty of a meadow or an unpretentious tree.

Which deadly sin did I commit to have to climb up to the Parthenon in Athens? I have a hard time navigating between the stands selling authentic junk and glass jewels made in China, mobbed by a crowd that couldn't care less about Greece and the gods now withdrawn to the inaccessible Olympus.

A blind man goes from one stand to another, begging. He is young, poorly dressed with a short beard, shy, his body language expressing divine gentleness. His closed eyes do not deceive: he embodies the new misery of that place. He does not remove the merchants, but he pities them. Homeless, the Messiah begs. Calvary is right here in its ugliness and money. He holds out his begging cup at his preferred spot, without a coat, a home or even a stone to put his head on. Here he is. What should I give him? Can he see that I recognize Him, that He has been revealed to me?

He gives me a blessing, Christ saves me. With closed eyelids, lucid, He understands my misery and my begging.

Phœbus and Boreas

The *Fables* of La Fontaine reveal an immemorial past in which our ancestors, whether believers in fetishism, totemism, or animism, had a vision of the world different from ours that has cut our souls off from the world's soul. We do not take the marvelous seriously, even though it could inspire ethnology, the history of religion and even the sciences themselves.

Phœbus and Boreas are not just the names of symbols for the sun and the Wind. They are not rhetorical tropes, for amusement or for poetry as learned critics explain, but name the world's soul under two aspects: the light shining or burning on the waves and the breeze whose strength is stupendous. Like everything living or non-living, like the world and me, the animist Traveler carries within himself the soul that attunes him to the Universe. His heart and arteries burn with heat while his skin may shiver from the cold; his legs run everywhere as fast as the wind like his horse's hoofs. He lives in the world, he is of the world; he is the world. The same soul, another body.

The Knight rushes body and soul into a world composed of Phœbus and Boreas, like his own soul. He experiences the presence of that soul, just as Eli in the book of Kings feels the presence of Yahweh: "There was a hurricane but the Lord was not in the hurricane…"

The weather improves and "after the fire, there was the sound of a light breeze." The moment has come to undress and naked, with a covered face, to hear the Lord, whose voice speaks through light and the breeze, through the *ruagh*, the spiritual wind.

Just as silly as the Judeo-Christian one, Æsop's fable remains polytheistic in a vaguely euhemerist way. What is more common and stupid than two males quarreling over their respective strength, like two small cockerels or street kids, like two politicians, gods of a cardboard Pantheon? Already in antiquity Æsop had lost the deep thoughts and the capacity for enthusiasm of our animistic fathers in ecstasy in the world's soul. The real value of its magic has been forgotten by our authors of fables. However, in his "Discours à Madame de La Sablière", La Fontaine says that a purified flame can give some idea of the soul. The moral of that fable is as follows: when you feel around you the divine charm coming from the gentle breeze and the shrouded sun, you will be saved from the wind in which Yahweh is not.

"And behold, the Lord passed by, and a great and strong wind rent the mountains, and brake in pieces the rocks before the Lord; but the Lord was not in the wind: and after the wind an earthquake; but the Lord was not in the earthquake: and after the earthquake, a fire; but the Lord was not in the fire: and after the fire a still small voice.

And it was so, when Elijah heard it, and he wrapped his face in his mantle and went out and stood in the entering of the cave. And behold, there came a voice unto him, and said…"

I, Kings, XIX, p 687. *King James version of the Holy Bible,* The Limited Editions Club, New York, 1935.

Softening sight until things are invivisble; softening
the wind until it becomes a light breeze, softening
sound until it becomes a whisper; lessening hearing as
close to silence as possible; softening the voice until
confession; softening the cold to warm yourself;
reduce the five senses to numbness; softening definite
sensation until ecstasy; moderating flashy colors until
they turn into visionary white… softening the hard and
the soft until the world is turned around.

La Fontaine's *Fables* are mostly about animals and rarely introduce
flora, people or things in the world. Here the Wind and the Sun
are quarreling over a traveler. Light and heat defeat noise and fury.
Violence achieves less than gentleness. Will softness win over
hardness and grace over gravity?

Francois Chauveau, Illustration for "Phœbus and Boreas" [the Wind and the
Sun], 1728 edition, private collection.

Jeremiah of Amsterdam

Revealed inside the Rijksmuseum: the mystical sun is shining over the prophet's head bathed in supernatural light. From the top of his white-haired head, the intense glow flows down his beard and forearm and leaves a shiny tear as a trace on the helmet that lies on top of the open coat.

A bit bent over, the silent meditating body is immersed in the same light that surrounds him. The intense light is reflected in the distant reddish flame that sets alight the earthly Jerusalem. A punctual sun ray emerging as though from an oven discreetly tears the painting, illuminates the silent room, shines on the city and its canals, and emerges from another world to save ours.

A visionary genius, Rembrandt shows the invisible. He shows not just the milky white of Vermeer's pot, or the blue of Van Gogh's skies, the mystical and secret serenity of Angelico's Annunciation that renders the divine visible; not only what we should see with our body's eyes but that which is seen only by the eyes of Watteau and Manet; not just the abstract law we understand with an intelligent glance and cries of Eureka; not only the philosopher's meditation in his room in front of the window at dawn: Rembrandt shows the mystery of existence, the world and our destiny. Here is divine fire.

Rembrandt's work reaches the level of prophetic vision in the mystical bedazzlement of the disciples of Emmaus who suddenly realize that their travel and table companion is the Risen One. He rises to Jeremiah's vision, but not the Jeremiah whose stone body is crying in the Moissac tympanum. In this painting he seems to be dozing with closing eyelids; he sees the supernatural that sees him. As if welded by molted iron, His brow is lit up with the nuclear white of the forge, the sum of all the world's colors.

What is painting? Transfiguration.

Few paintings can be considered among the most beautiful in the world, like this one. Brilliant and discreet, the luxurious splendor of the visible colors return to a secret intimacy where we and the prophet lament human misery.

Rembrandt, *Jeremiah Lamenting the Destruction of Jerusalem*, 1630, Rijksmuseum, Amsterdam.

Transfiguration

The divine shines – *dius* like *dies* – the light of day.

"The eye in which I see God is the same eye in which
God sees me. My eye and God's eye are one and the
same eye, one and the same vision, one and the
same knowledge and one and the same love."
Maître Eckhart, Sermon 12, in *Traités et sermons*,
op. cit., p. 299.
He chooses Peter, Paul and John to take them to an
isolated spot at the top of a high mountain. There
He is transfigured before them: "His face shone like
the sun, and his clothes became white as light."
(Matthew, 17, 2, Standard English Version). We tell
him, let us pitch three tents and stay here in the
company of Moses and the prophet Elijah. Dazzled
by your radiance we will live there for the rest of
our lives. Alas! We went down again.

To paint, to fake. In geometry, the *figure*
drawn on the board is not the same
as the one reasoned about. Like *fiction*,
it imitates or represents. Similarly,
the painter fakes more than he paints
in trying to show what eyes don't see.
There are three levels: people standing,
the apostles and then finally, the flying
trio. Raphael tries to unfold the hidden
relationship between what is seen and
the things themselves, between visible
representation and hidden reality.

Raphael, *The Transfiguration*, 1519,
Vatican Museum.

Signature

The queen and the king beat the drum to summon the
best painter of the realm to their thrones. One was selected in
a competition. The winner appeared at the court and asked what his
mission was. The sovereigns said: "It is to paint the most beautiful painting
in the world." The artist accepted.

He asked for seven years and seven workdays, seven female assistants, seven male
assistants and a workshop in the mountains, seven kilometers from the capital. This was
granted. At the end of the term, the queen and king requested the painting. The painter
asked for another delay of seven years and seven days. It was granted. Again a request
followed by another postponement: the same scene happened seven times seven years.

At the end of half a century of this process, a golden coach appeared at the steps of the
palace, drawn by seven chestnut horses, preceded by seven women assistants dressed in
white robes and seven male assistants dressed in black. The painter got out of the carriage
with the painting and presented it facing the throne surrounded by the court. All admired
the work for seven times seven hours. It was truthfully the most beautiful painting in
the world.

Then the queen raised her arm and with her finger pointed to a minute space
where she said there remained some defect. Then one saw the humiliated
artist walk in small steps to the painting, getting closer and closer until
he could touch it and then suddenly enter the small recess and
disappear, as if snatched up by this magnetic well.
He was never seen again.

The arrows show the way, while the circles
imitate the dizzying whirlwind. These two
structures explain the double and contradictory
meaning of the preposition *towards*, designating
movement and rotation. So-called abstract
painting has suddenly become figurative.

Giacomo Balla, *Vertigo of Life*, 1929, private collection.

Copyrights

IMPRIM'VERT®

Printed in France by Gibert Clarey, Chambray-lès-Tours
Dépôt légal : avril 2015
N° d'édition : 74650906-01